On a Teleconference No One Knows You're a Dog

45 Marketing Hacks for Startups

Michael J. Carden

Copyright © 2018 Michael J. Carden.

All rights reserved.

ISBN-10: 1985211017
ISBN-13: 978-1985211018

Cover Art Heidi Eger.

For Molly and Jack

Contents

	Acknowledgments	i
1	Imperfect Marketing	1
2	Clarity Beats Everything	13
3	Tables with Skirts and Other Low Points	23
4	Marketing Umami	35
5	Ladies and Gentlemen!	55
6	Brave New World	72
7	White-Coat Marketing	92
8	The Pac-Man Conundrum	109
9	Sales Isn't Magic	123
10	Life's a Riot with Spy Vs. Spy	137
11	Brushing Your Teeth While Eating Cake	157
12	Schmarketing	180

Acknowledgements

Most of this book was written in Tejakula, Bali, Indonesia, and without being surrounded by the warmth and kindness of the people of Tejakula and the beauty of Indonesia I am sure that this book would have had a very different vibe.

The list of people who stimulated the learning captured in this book is far too long to call out everyone, but many thanks must go to Kai Crow, Karen Rayner and Shelly Drader who made up our first marketing team at Sonar6, and Mark Hellier, John Holt and Pete Weaver, without whom there would have been no Sonar6.

This book happened with the help, guidance, and collective shoulder of Mary Ellen Slater, Beth Colvin, Steve Masters and the rest of the team at Rep Cap, Laurie Ruettimann, and Anna Livesey — without whom there would have been lots of words but no story.

Lastly, special thanks to Carli Eger, who read every word almost as soon as I spat it onto the page, provided critique, cups of tea, and the motivation to finish the fucker.

1.
Imperfect Marketing

'Msitakes' Are Golden

It was a Tuesday. I got to work early because Tuesday was the day we sent out the newsletter to the sales prospects for our human resources software. Newsletter. Prospects. Human resources. I can imagine your eyes glazing over. But that's what we did — every Tuesday we emailed people, tens of thousands of them, with a personalized email, a slick newsletter and an invitation to our webinar. It was a key part of our marketing strategy.

That Tuesday I was distracted. I was in the middle of a fight with my future ex-wife — something about the children — and just autopiloting through the morning routine. The marketing team had worked out that Tuesday was the best day to send our email — highest open rates, best click-through. So Monday we got everything primed. Tuesday I got in early. Checked everything was right. Hit send.

Then my heart lurched. My brain went "Shit! You've really

screwed up."

I don't remember the exact subject line of that email, but I remember the team and I had spent a lot of time discussing it — specifically, whether it should have an exclamation mark. Eventually we sent it to A/B testing. The testing showed more people opened it without the exclamation mark.

A lot of effort goes into a decent marketing email. A/B testing helps fine-tune the content. You send two subtly different versions of a message ("A" and "B") to a sample of your database and see which performs better. Then you do it over and over, improving and refining each time.

At Sonar6 we prided ourselves on the quality of our email marketing. We won awards. Part of this was that we tested EVERYTHING. This particular Tuesday the email had cornball cartoon characters representing clichéd employees and employers. There was "office party guy," "entitled millennial" and "socially awkward engineer." You get the idea. They didn't appeal to me, but they'd performed well in testing, so out they went.

One of my Tuesday morning jobs was to check that the link in the email to our prospects database (our list of names) was working. So far it always had been. So I sort of … ignored that piece. I really wanted to get a coffee and the clock was ticking. I hit send.

I sent out an email with the opening line "Dear {FirstName LastName}." That's actually what it said. Marketers will feel my pain. It's the marketing equivalent of the dream where you arrive at school in only your underpants.

I saw the text at the top of the email just as I hit send and as it was disappearing off my screen, down the pipes toward the screens of thousands of prospects. My brain kicked in milliseconds too late. I panicked. And in my panic to stop the email, I sent everyone on the list the same bust email again.

I had let the team down. My phone started ringing with my workmates saying "What the fuck?" My inbox started filling with potential customers saying "duh, Michael J. Carden, marketing FAIL!"

So I sent ANOTHER email to everyone on the list. Hastily put together. No nice graphics. Apologizing for my mistake and promising that the webinar would be better than the email. I remember the subject line of that email very clearly: "Oops, I screwed up."

And here's the thing. That apology email became the best-performing email we'd ever produced. That week we signed up 10 times more people for the webinar than ever before. *Ten times.*

So while I was getting hammered at the office for sloppy work, I also seemingly struck marketing gold. I was the Forrest Gump of marketing. An email written in haste with no research, no graphics, *no testing at all* outperformed our award-winning marketing by an order of magnitude.

As the day wore on and the success of the apology email became clear in the record-breaking sign-up stats for the webinar, my whole understanding of marketing started unraveling. Tuesday was collapsing in on itself. I left work early. I knew something important had happened and I wanted to try to figure it out.

So I went to a bar.

On a Teleconference No One Knows You're a Dog

In the early days of our startup, when there were only three of us, we had this narrow, upstairs office near the center of Auckland, New Zealand's capital. It was ramshackle. You had to go through a series of abandoned rooms to get to it, and it had holes in the walls that looked like they'd been made with fists. There had been an artist working there before us, so the floor was splattered with paint and everything always smelled slightly of solvents.

But on a teleconference that doesn't matter, right?

I was sitting at the big communal desk that I shared with my co-founder Mark Hellier. Mark's one of those guys who's a master of several things, but his real strength is that he's a generalist. He can do almost anything about 80 percent as well as an expert. He can fix your car, tailor you a suit or kayak a waterfall. With only a YouTube clip for research, Mark can do an adequate job of anything. Bill Reichert from Garage Technology Ventures said all startups need an optimist, a pessimist and an engineer: someone to say the glass is half full, someone to say it's half empty and an engineer to point out that the glass is the wrong size. At Sonar6, Mark was our engineer.

This particular morning Mark and I were on a teleconference trying to convince a potential customer in the U.S. that our technical infrastructure was secure enough to house their sensitive HR data. Our desk was up against a window that faced a busy street: Nelson Street, right by a freeway off-ramp, with six lanes of cars making the rapid adjustment from commute to central city chaos. The intersection was always noisy, and on this day the noise was worse than usual because of a big rainstorm.

Partway through the teleconference, as the CIO on the other end lobbed data-encryption questions at Mark, the wind picked up dramatically. Rain pelted the window. After a few moments of this violence a huge crack appeared across the windowpane. Mark, unperturbed, continued answering the distant CIO's queries. Water ran through the crack and onto the desk. Mark, still talking, still calm, started moving the phone and all the company's computer gear off the desk, out of reach of the growing puddle. I climbed up onto the desk with an empty pizza box to try to seal the window. More questions about the quality of our infrastructure were diligently answered, with Mark now trying to prevent water from flowing into the power sockets and me standing on the desk, trying to protect us from the elements with a square of cheesy, greasy cardboard.

Then the window gave way completely. A massive shard of glass fell out and smashed onto the pavement below. Oh. My. God. I peered out. Fortunately no one had been directly underneath, but evidently someone was nearby: Through the now-much-louder noise of the rain blowing straight into the office and the traffic roaring up, I could hear someone yelling about falling glass.

Unfazed, Mark realized this had gone far enough: "Hey, so, if there aren't any more questions we might wrap this up; unfortunately someone else has this meeting room booked and they are outside," he said cheerfully.

And that right there is a unifying feature of all startups. You try to appear bigger and more organized than you could possibly be. Have you ever caught yourself saying "I'll put you through to someone in the support team," even though you know there is only Dominik, you share a desk and you're going to physically pass him the phone? That's what I'm talking about.

Covering up the madness you work in isn't necessarily a bad thing (in fact it's often the only sane choice), but it starts a habit of speaking with a voice that's askew. You start saying "we" when you mean "I." You aim for a slick, professional, corporate tone in your dealings with clients and possible clients. Then your marketing gets infected with the same speak. And that's where things go wrong. Or perhaps not so much wrong as blah.

Who Makes Your Cookies?

So let's leave our first office with the water flooding in and return to the Tuesday of the bust email. I left work and was sitting in my local bar trying to digest the day — how my bungled email and follow-up apology had so dramatically outperformed our slick marketing efforts. Sure, I struck marketing gold this one time, but relying on future mistakes didn't seem like a viable strategy.

If you had asked me about eureka moments before that day, I think I would have said they were fakes — Newton being hit on the head with an apple, Paul McCartney waking up with "Yesterday" already written, Art Fry realizing that his shitty glue could be used for Post-It notes — nicely marketed moments that were actually years of hard work. But as I sat there toying with my beer I was struck by a revelation.

I grabbed a coaster and scribbled it down:

It is easy to ignore marketing but hard to ignore people.

People who saw that apology email didn't see it as marketing content. The subject line made them feel they were interacting with another human being — a slightly stupid human being, but a real person nevertheless. *That's* why they responded.

We're all adept at filtering. The world is a big, busy place with lots going on, so we just focus on the stuff that's relevant at the time, like preventing our offspring from being eaten by lions, or stopping the rain from wrecking all our computer gear, or getting our morning coffee. We have to filter unimportant, unnecessary things — like marketing. Every person whose attention you want has a well-developed marketing filter. This filter is so strong that people sometimes literally don't see stuff they subconsciously identify as marketing.[1]

Which means successful marketing has to start by breaking through that marketing filter. One way to achieve that is by connecting on a human-to-human level — just as I had accidentally done.

Here's another example. There's a company in my neighborhood that makes cookies. Their tagline is "We believe you deserve the world's best cookies." I'm sure a lot of thought went into creating that line, but it just looks *so much* like marketing — and it's very easy to ignore. That "We believe" at the beginning immediately falls into a category of marketing communication I think of as *"Things Humans Never Say."* That's a bad place to start when you're trying to make a human-to-human connection. Starting a sentence with "we believe" is not believable at all: Nobody gets any sense of the people behind that "we." And "the world's best" — that's a big claim, and not one that has any sense of appropriate human scale in it. I like cookies, and I'd rather have a good one than a bad one. But they're only cookies. I'd probably settle for the best cookies available within 10 minutes of my house. I don't think I'm after the best cookies in the world. So while "We believe you deserve the world's best cookies" is slick, it's not good, in the sense of "likely to be effective."

Imagine instead: "Karen, Kai and Shelly make our cookies." Just that. Just a simple, matter-of-fact statement. It's not slick, but it's human — and thus *much* more likely to break through people's marketing filter.

---

[1] This phenomenon is also called "selective attention." For a demonstration of the power of your mind to filter out information that doesn't seem relevant, Google the phrase "selective attention test" and watch the YouTube video of people passing a basketball.

Nothing You Know Is Useful Here

After Sonar6 was acquired and I extricated myself, I went on a vacation. A long vacation. Eventually I wound up in Marrakech, Morocco. In the center of the medina (the walled medieval town) is Jemaa el-Fna Square, and this is where I found myself on my first evening, as the desert sun set and the air began to fill with smoke from street vendors barbecuing meat.

Marrakech is wedged between the edge of the desert and the foothills of the Atlas Mountains. It has long been a trade hub. For centuries, people from the surrounding area have come into Marrakech once a month to trade and buy supplies. If you're only in town for a few days a month, you want to party — and if you're going to party in Marrakech, you go to Jemaa el-Fna Square. It's one of the busiest squares in all of Africa, and I suspect it has been since it was built in the 11th century. It's a standing-invite party that's been going for 1,000 years.

But it's not the sort of party that I'm used to. As soon as I entered the throng — and it really was a throng — a discombobulating array of sights overwhelmed me. Snake charmers. Storytellers. Goats' heads being pulled out of boiling vats, cleaved in half, then served with plastic forks. Acrobats. Scorpion eaters. Bowls of steaming snails. A cacophony of musicians. I felt like I had wandered into the bar scene from "Star Wars."

A woman grabbed my arm, looking like she was about to jab me with the syringe she held in her other hand. "Henna tattoo," she explained, as I pulled away in fright, only to be confronted with a man wielding a fearsome set of pliers and displaying a tray of extracted molars — presumably intended as testaments to his skill.

As I moved through the crowd, I came across a ring of

people. I pushed toward the front to see what they were watching. I was struck by the diversity of the crowd: Berbers, and Bedouins, all excitedly waving their hands and shouting. I could see fists held tight, full of cash, and money changing hands, like people were betting on something. Finally, standing on my tiptoes, I could see into the ring of people. There were two nervous-looking kids in boxing gloves.

Everything I learned in my life up to this point was not useful here.

It's a strangely liberating feeling to accept that things you thought were universal actually only work in the narrow confines of your previous experience. I'd been to plenty of parties before. But never this kind of party.

I started writing this book back at my hotel that first night in Marrakech. On the rooftop, under the stars, I riffed on this simple question: What makes marketing in startups so different? What could I put down on paper about what I learned?

A Startup Marketing Adventure

This is a book about marketing for startups. It's also an adventure story. Almost all of the experiences that shape my understanding of marketing happened when I left my marketing job at Hewlett-Packard to go off-grid and build a company from scratch with a couple of guys I had met mountain biking. When I told my family my plan they looked at me as if I'd just said "I've decided to be a pirate."

The company I helped found was called Sonar6, and we started in Auckland. Over six years, we grew until we had offices and clients around the world. Then we were acquired by one of our large U.S.-based competitors. Before I started at Sonar6 I worked in marketing in a series of large corporates, culminating in my time with HP. Those are the companies where I learned how to be a marketer. Naturally, I applied what I knew at Sonar6. It didn't work.

I now think it didn't work because the rules of startups are completely different from the rules of established businesses, and the discipline of marketing was developed by established businesses.

Everything I learned in my life up to this point was not useful here.

There are two things that, by definition, apply to all startups: They are small and they are new. When we started Sonar6, I thought "small" and "new" were negative things, because everything I learned in marketing up to that point said that big was good, that heritage had value. So our marketing tried to hide those two truths.

Which is the opposite of what we should've done.

Small companies can be irreverent and targeted because they don't need to appeal to everyone. New companies can iterate their offerings quickly because they don't have a whole lot of existing customers to upset. If you're small and new, you can make your products feel rare and unique. These are all things that big companies struggle with.

Most importantly, small new companies can do something that big established companies find almost impossible: They can build human-to-human connections that break through people's marketing filters. Think about it this way. A startup is a small band of people, and a small band of people is much more likely to make a human connection than a large corporation is. *Human-to-human connection is the key to startup marketing.*

When I proposed the tagline "Karen, Kai and Shelly make our cookies," those weren't just random names. Karen, Kai and Shelly were the first members of the Sonar6 marketing team. Respectively, a crafty genius, a downhill mountain biker and my future ex-wife. We were a ragtag bunch, but, my God, we did some kick-ass marketing.

"Hack" is a good illustration of how quickly language changes. As a verb, its meanings range from chopping vegetation to gaining illegal access to computer systems to playing bad golf. But when I tell you that Karen, Kai, Shelly and I spent our days hacking marketing, I mean none of those things. What I mean is that we broke and remade what we knew about marketing so that it worked in a startup. The marketing that came out of our little band at Sonar6 was resource-constrained and sometimes ugly, but nearly always effective.

In this book, I put down what we learned along the way.

Startup Marketing Hacks #1-3

1. Connection, not perfection, is the goal.

Most marketing departments strive for perfection, to make every piece of content as perfect as possible. But perfection is impersonal, not human, and is easy to filter out. To make a connection you need to act like what you are — a human. Even imperfections and screw-ups can work to your advantage if you use them as an opportunity to connect with your audience on a human-to-human level.

2. Let them know who makes your cookies.

Our brains get bombarded daily with marketing content. We're all adept at only noticing the things that seem relevant — our marketing filter at work. An abstract "we" making "the best cookies in the world" doesn't even touch that filter. Karen, Kai and Shelly, hands sticky with dough, making cookies right here, for you, is much more likely to get through.

Whenever you create a piece of marketing content, ask these questions: *Would I filter this if it wasn't mine? Is there something human about the content I've just made?*

3. *Nothing you know is useful here.*

The rules of marketing learned in established businesses are not useful for startups. You don't have the time or the resources for it, and even if you did it wouldn't work for you.

Startups have the ability to appear like a small band of humans figuring it out as they go along *because that's what they are*. Big companies can't do that. That's the advantage you need to learn to use.

2.
Clarity Beats Everything

Great Businesses Are Salad-Proof
If you drew a pyramid of the economics of tech in 2006 it would look something this: The U.S. had the biggest tech economy. California was the biggest chunk. Within California, Silicon Valley dominated. All the big Silicon Valley venture capital firms were on Sand Hill Road in Menlo Park. And the Sand Hill Road VC that had done the biggest deals was Sequoia Capital. Apple, Oracle, Google — all were backed by Sequoia.

We were meeting with Michael Goguen, and with a mouth full of salad, he waved impatiently at the screen as if to say "Come on, show me what you've got." We were in the office of Sequoia Capital, pitching for our Series A funding. We'd exchanged pleasantries in one of those lopsided, startup-folk ways. It was Friday, and he was going snowmobiling in Montana for the weekend. At a resort which he managed to mention he owned. I said I loved Montana, but I didn't mention I'd never been. He was sorry he had to eat his lunch during the pitch, but one of Sequoia's portfolio companies, YouTube, had been acquired the previous day by Google, so they'd been out late to celebrate. I wanted to be him, not me.

It was John Holt and me in the meeting. John was one of my fellow co-founders at Sonar6. Born into a family of boys on the South Island of New Zealand, John grew up protecting his dinner. He's quite possibly the most competitive person I've ever met. If we were going to the same place in separate cars, it would always be a race. Once, racing to a restaurant in Corte Madera, California, I managed to slip through a light before it turned red at the freeway off-ramp, so John was well behind me. I was parking in the Cheesecake Factory lot when John careened his rental over the top of a traffic island, leapt out of his still-running car and sprinted to the front door of the restaurant, shouting "first to touch the door wins." You get the picture. That guy.

The corollary to John's hyper-competitive personality is that no challenge is insurmountable. He had this expression: "We're not here to fuck mice," and he applied it liberally. We had a piece of beta HR software that was held together with tape, we had only two customers (both in New Zealand) and he had arranged for us to pitch to Sequoia to raise $5 million. Every startup needs a John Holt.

So there we were, and just as we started into our PowerPoint the Sequoia guy spilled his entire salad box into his lap. He cursed. He started to try to clean himself up with napkins. He looked up from his lap for a second to say "Sorry about that guys, just keep going," then went back to focusing on getting the ranch dressing off his trousers. He got up and got bottled water to use. Then he left the room briefly to get a cloth. "Keep going guys, I'm still listening."

Against this backdrop of salad chaos, we went through our pitch — carefully explaining how the software that we had built helped CEOs and HR people build an inventory of their talent, recognize their high-performers, identify areas of the business where ... *blah blah blah*. At the end, he asked one question:

"So, what does your product actually do?"

John and I both probably started babbling about McKinsey and the war for talent and all of the other things that we had in our usual spiel. But we had already failed. Great businesses are salad-proof: simple enough to understand through the chaos of day-to-day life.

If you can't explain your business to someone cleaning ranch dressing off his crotch, it'll never fly in a marketplace crowded with marketing messages.

"Gone in Sixty Seconds"

The movie "Gone in Sixty Seconds" is generally considered one of the worst of producer Jerry Bruckheimer's efforts. His others — including "Top Gun," "Bad Boys," "The Rock," "Con Air" and "Armageddon" — aren't really a list of critics' choices, but "Gone in Sixty Seconds," with RottenTomatoes.com score of 24 percent, has a view of the field. It's basically like watching someone else play "Grand Theft Auto." However, like all Bruckheimer movies, it was a decent box office performer.

There's a rumor that when the movie was pitched to Bruckheimer, there was no script, no storyboards, just a single line: *A gang of thieves have to steal 50 luxury cars in 24 hours*. And that's it — there's the beauty of "Gone in Sixty Seconds."

The premise is so simple, so explainable, so appealing,

that the whole ecosystem gets it immediately. Whether it's a studio deciding to invest millions or a suburban couple on a date night choosing a movie, that single line connects, and that connection turns into good business.

When we started Sonar6, we were very uncertain how to describe what we did. We knew that the difference between organizations that prospered and those that did poorly was often how well they managed people. We also knew that people were the most expensive resource in a business. Add those things together and it's obvious that businesses would be willing to spend money on managing their people better. The problem was trying to convince anyone that our software — any software, in fact — was going to help.

We started by demonstrating that there was a lot going on with our product. We made it look complex and scientific. I even wrote a paper called "Talent Science: The emerging science of people management." Ugh.

It's a common trap. Most startups have a chip on their shoulder about being small. One thing they do to make themselves seem bigger is to describe themselves in complicated ways. Because complicated means bigger and smarter.

That trip to Sequoia started a sea change for Sonar6. It crystallized something desperately missing — simplicity. When we started Sonar6 we were a "talent-management system, to help corporations get an accurate inventory of all of their talent; to understand who were their stars, and who were the underperformers." By the end of that year we were "At last, performance reviews that don't suck."

Simple is better. If something is simple people are more likely to understand it, and more likely to connect. So while our product was sophisticated software that helped businesses understand the capabilities of all their people, our go-to-market message was a simple one. We made performance reviews that didn't suck.

People could relate to this. The opening dialog would go like this:

"Does your business do performance reviews?"

"Yes."

"Are they good?"

"No. Everyone hates them."

"Well, we can fix that for you."

The conversation was underway. Now we could introduce all the other amazing things that we could do for them, which would hopefully convince them to buy from us and not our competition.

All markets are crowded. The internet is a very crowded space. Everybody is ignoring your stuff. Even if you manage to get someone's attention, you only have it for a few seconds. Having a business built around a simple message makes all the difference.

Find Your Dolphin

The Māui dolphin is a very small, very rare subspecies of dolphin. It was discovered as a separate species in 2002 when genetic analysis showed it wasn't just a regional variant of the more common Hector's dolphin. It's estimated there are 55 adult Māui dolphins left. They're only found in the waters off the west coast of the North Island of New Zealand, in an area that was a marine sanctuary intended to protect them. In mid-2014 the New Zealand government opened the sanctuary for oil drilling.

Opposition political parties saw an opportunity to attack, and by the time of the general election later that year, a vote for the incumbent government had become a vote for the extinction of the Māui dolphin. Even to someone with only moderate understanding of the issues, this seems like an oversimplification, but it's exactly that kind of simple symbolism that works so effectively as marketing.

The environment is a huge and complex system, intertwined with the economy and our everyday life and activities. In New Zealand in 2014, there were certainly more significant environmental issues than those 55 dolphins. Lots of issues were objectively much bigger and more important, but just too hard to explain. So the political marketers found a symbol, and an easy-to-grasp, salad-defying message — "this government kills dolphins" — and they focused on that.

If you want to understand the leading edge of marketing, look to politics. Look to the spin doctors. Symbols are the best weapon in their arsenal. In the world of politics, symbols stick better than drawn-out arguments and appeals to logic. It's the same in the world of startup marketing. Symbols stick.

The market won't grasp the details of what you do, or be interested. This is especially true if you're doing something that hasn't been done before. The easiest way to simplify your marketing is to look for the symbol of the problem your business solves.

When Sonar6 said "At last, performance reviews that don't suck," we were pinpointing a symbol.[2] Even though we built complicated software that solved the complicated problem of people management, what we talked about was one resonant symbol: the shitty performance review.

Simplifying things often means that some of the

---

[2] Another favorite example, Silvercar, is an Austin, Texas-based car-rental business whose point of difference is renting only one model of car: a new silver Audi A4. CEO Luke Schneider describes how this solves one of the major frustrations of car renters — not knowing what car you will get — in the brilliantly symbolic phrase "No more PT Cruiser roulette."

accuracy will be lost. But you have to be OK with that. The rule is: As long as you are trading accuracy for clarity, it's OK. If John and I had walked into that meeting with Sequoia and said, "We're Sonar6. We fix the broken performance review," we would have nailed it, salad chaos or not.

Let's Play Telephone

Remember the kids' game where one child is whispered a phrase and then they have to whisper what they heard to another child, and so on in a long line? We called it Telephone. At the end, you compare what the last kid in the line heard versus what was originally whispered, and it's normally pretty different.

Universally, word of mouth is considered the most effective marketing. One person tells another about your product, and so on, authentically, without intervention or cost to you. It's basically the same as our kids' game.

Once you've played Telephone for a bit, you realize that the more complicated the starting phrase is, the more it will get twisted along the chain for hilarious results. Simple phrases just get passed along the chain pretty much unchanged. Where's the fun in that?

The takeaway is this: If your marketing message is complicated, word of mouth just ceases to work. As soon as one person describes to a friend what your business does, the message is probably already pretty different from what you dreamed up — and a few people later it's unrecognizable. This is a good test: Explain your business to a stranger; later, get them to explain it back to you.

This is a core reason why businesses that are easy to explain outperform ones that aren't. A simple message can move around the ecosystem efficiently, without intervention.[3]

On Message, Right off the Bike

Te Mata Peak is a 400-meter-high (about 1,300 feet) limestone ridge in Hawke's Bay, New Zealand. The summit access road is narrow and winds up several kilometers of steep switchbacks. It's popular with cyclists in summer, but I visited in late winter. Driving up, I spotted only a single mountain biker.

I passed the mountain biker on one of the rare straights, and thought little of it other than commenting to my companion that it looked like hard work. We reached the top and had a very short walk in the wind before the cold got the best of us.

As we headed back to the car, the cyclist rounded the final bend leading to the summit. He was breathing hard, as you'd expect, but he also seemed surprisingly casual as he cycled right up to us. He dismounted and took off his helmet.

"Mike!" he exclaimed. "Have I told you about Pacific Fibre?"

It was Rod Drury. Rod is my benchmark for a successful tech entrepreneur. Now mostly known as CEO of Xero, a company with the crisp tagline of "online accounting software that's easy to love" and a multibillion-dollar market cap, Rod is the person whom I first heard describe the serial nature of entrepreneurship — you start one

---

[3] A good example of this difference is the historical valuations of the cloud-based storage giants Dropbox and Box, the former positioned simply as "file storage in the cloud," the latter with more complicated enterprise positioning. Despite being ostensibly similar, Dropbox has typically been valued at five times the value of Box.

company, make it go, then take what you've made in dollars and knowledge and turn it into another company. One of his projects at that time was Pacific Fibre, a hugely ambitious trans-Pacific telecommunications cable business. Here he was, straight off the bike, heart pumping, face pink, giving me the quick rundown on why a $400 million cable project was so important.

It was astounding, but also utterly characteristic — right off the bike, without even a pause for breath, the guy was completely on message.

Clarity allows you to be understood regardless of the circumstances and context. I didn't need a PowerPoint presentation and a complicated spiel to understand Pacific Fibre. A two-minute conversation on a windy hilltop was sufficient.

Startup Marketing Hacks #4-7

4. Be salad-proof.

Imagine everyone who ever hears about your business will be scrubbing ranch dressing out of their trousers at the same time as you're talking to them. Does your message get through? Almost all great startups are easily explained.

Don't fall into the trap of thinking that appearing complicated means you seem bigger. You'll just appear small and confused.

5. Find your dolphin.

In all your marketing, from tagline to content, try to find the things that symbolize the problem you're addressing, and focus on those. Symbols stick.

If what you do is too complex to explain simply then just explain part of it. Once you have someone's attention, you can always expand on the details.

6. *The Telephone test.*

A business that's super easy to understand has a much higher chance of success. The test: Explain your business to someone. Leave it a day, then get them to explain it back to you.

7. *On message, right off the bike.*

Your message should be straightforward enough that you can huff it out, full of enthusiasm and clarity, the second you climb off your bike on top of a mountain.

3.
Tables with Skirts and Other Low Points

Everyone Remembers a Really Dirty Deck
When Sonar6 first began, I, like many other founders of early-stage startups, was still taking odd jobs to bring in a bit of cash. A contact from my previous role offered me a gig giving breakfast-time marketing strategy talks to small-business owners across Canada. Many lessons have been learned on the wide, cold prairies of Alberta. A few of them turn out to be relevant to startup marketing.

The small-business owners would arrive at some ungodly hour (the sure sign of a successful person is their ability to get up earlier than everybody else). They'd pour themselves the bad coffee and eat the greasy croissants and network like demons. Then there'd be this big, noisy setup where the sponsor would be thanked and I'd get introduced with the preamble "all the way from New Zealand," as if distance traveled somehow implied capability. *He's all the way from where? He must be good.*

Then I'd go on and be … mediocre. Honestly. I got the work because of my marketing strategy experience, not because I was great at enthralling groups of prairie folk who owned gyms or car dealerships or spa pool installation businesses and who'd been up since 5 a.m. In the first couple of sessions I wheeled out some slides about Richard Branson and Virgin and tried to be inspirational. It was pretty flat.

By the third session — in Lethbridge, Alberta — I had to try something different. I decided to get someone from the audience up on stage with me and ask them about their business. After much cajoling one guy agreed to come up. His colleagues cheered and I started thinking this might actually work. He owned an outdoor cedar construction business. Pergolas. Gazebos. Decks. I asked him a bit about the business, what some of the challenges were, and we got to talking about ongoing customer relationships.

"Do you just construct or do you maintain as well?" I asked. He didn't get what I meant, so I expanded.

"Well, say I had a dirty deck, could your guys come around and clean it?" He now looked confused, almost nervous. The audience had gone quiet. Very quiet.

Let me pause here. I am a New Zealander. I don't think of myself as having a particularly strong accent, but I talk like a New Zealander, and apparently when I say "deck" North Americans hear "dick."

I could tell the cedar construction man didn't understand me, but I wasn't sure why. It was a pretty simple question. So I did what everyone talking to a foreigner does when they're not getting through. I repeated myself — louder.

"WHAT IF I HAD A REALLY DIRTY DECK, COULD SOME OF YOUR GUYS COME AROUND AND WATERBLAST MY DECK?"

The cedar man was actually going red. The polite Canadian audience shuffled uncomfortably in their seats. I knew something was badly wrong, but, like everyone else in the room, I couldn't really put my finger on what it was. Until the production assistant walked on stage, calmly took the microphone from me, and explained to the audience that the problem was my accent. People started laughing. In fact, people started cheering. People stood up and clapped, they were so enthused. I got a fucking standing ovation! In Lethbridge, Alberta. For saying "dick."

I wasn't professional but I was memorable. Gym owners, car dealers and spa pool installers in Lethbridge probably still talk about me. No set of slides about Richard Branson, no matter how slick, could have been as memorable as me, shouting in my weird accent about my dirty deck.

Get Out from Under My Skirt and into the Box

All little worlds have their big events. In the world of HR software, the big event every year is the HR Tech conference in Chicago. That sounds like a fun day out, doesn't it? Major software vendors spend a quarter of a million dollars each to have a dominant presence there: elaborate customer parties, carefully managed media events, huge multilevel booths with Cirque du Soleil acrobats (I'm not making this up). The first year I went, I wandered around the massive show floor like someone from a farming village magically transported to New York City, muttering "they sure don't have buildings like this back home."

Even the smallest booth — 10 feet by 10 feet — was more than we could afford that first year. Instead Mark, John and I went to all the parties, hung out in the press room and tweeted like crazy people. We wore and handed out T-shirts and stickers with slogans that poked gentle fun at HR practices: "I met expectations." "Should never have added my boss on Facebook." "I heart HR ladies." Before long our T-shirts and stickers were everywhere. We even posted mock job ads in the bathrooms. We hadn't spent any money with the actual trade show, but our presence was obvious.

We did get into some trouble. Before the show started we tweeted about setting up our magnificent booth. It was early days for social media, so the organizers hired a consultancy to help build the show's social media presence. These guys were retweeting everything — including our posts about testing our laser light show. They started seriously hyping us, encouraging attendees to check out the Sonar6 booth. Which, of course, didn't actually exist.

When attendees went looking for us and couldn't find us, questions started being asked. The organizers heard about us handing out T-shirts (without paying the show's fee for handing out T-shirts) and decided to track us down. They found us in the registration area, where John was swapping out the official sponsored pens with stacks of "I heart HR ladies" Sonar6 pens. John's not a small guy and he goes nowhere quietly; watching him being "escorted" off the show floor really is one of my favorite memories of the entire Sonar6 journey.

The next year HR Tech rolled around again and we needed to be involved. Bill Kutik, HR Tech's boss at the time, is (despite living in a very pleasant part of Connecticut) an archetypal New Yorker: fiercely intelligent, spiritually generous and grumpy as all hell. He agreed a bit of drama and intrigue was needed for a show like his to really work. Sonar6 fit into this. But he also reminded us that we were a startup, not a bunch of upstarts. So we decided to play by the rules. Sort of.

We paid for a 10-by-10-foot booth. And in it we put a really big brown cardboard box.

Most people who buy a 10-by-10-foot booth do the same thing: put up plastic signs printed with their company name; cover the table legs with a white table skirt; put a fish bowl on the table and offer you the chance to win an iPad if you put your business card in the bowl. They lay out all of their paraphernalia and then they try to make eye contact with everyone who passes. As soon as they make eye contact, they pounce. It's awful.

We just put this huge cardboard box in our area. We'd cut a hole in the side of the box for people to go into. It was a pretty low opening though, so they had to duck to get in. Inside there was a video playing telling people just how damn fun we were. When anyone visited the cardboard box we handed them a marker pen and let them write and draw on the box. Someone wrote "Go Bears." Before you knew it there were sports debates raging on the outside of our box. When people asked us why we had a box, not a booth, we explained that we were a software company and the best place to learn about software was on the internet, not at a trade show. Then we handed them a pen.

Eventually an organizer came up and told us we were making a mockery of the show. A very angry woman from another vendor chipped in, saying we were bringing the tone down. They looked like they wanted us to pack up our cardboard box and go back to New Zealand. John pointed out that, because of Chicago's unionized workforce, even putting a cardboard box up had cost five grand. Eventually they left us alone.

Meanwhile, the box was creating a buzz. People were interested. They were coming looking for us and our big box. Our un-booth went on to win attendees' choice for best booth. We generated more press and blog coverage than the big-budget vendors who dominated the space. Sure, some people hated us, but others *loved* us. Hold that thought...

At HR Tech 2009, Sonar6 were disruptors! In startup world, that's some kind of holy grail in itself. But, to be honest, confrontation makes me anxious.

The cardboard box idea came from Kai Crow. Mark and I had met Kai mountain biking, right at the very start of Sonar6. Kai was a graphic designer who recently moved from a small town to big-city Auckland. We got to talking at the dirt jumps where Mark and I would hang out some evenings after work. Kai needed work and we needed website graphics, so he came and did some contracting. We soon discovered that Kai is one of those rare people who can be both wildly creative and deeply analytical, often in the same sentence. He went on to become our marketing manager, and to this day is one of the most gifted marketing practitioners I've met.

Kai always speaks slowly and purposefully. I remember, during one discussion about the cardboard box, I told Kai that the whole concept made me nervous. I was worried about the possible negative reaction.

"Mike," he said in his deliberate way, "if you want to be a disruptor, you are going to have to be OK with being disruptive." In hindsight, it's so obvious. Game-changers change the game. If the game is "the vendor with the biggest trade show stand wins" and you can't afford to have the biggest trade show stand, then you need to change the game.

Trade show tables with skirts and fishbowls epitomize professional over interesting — and they're a game you can't win. As a startup you need to get out of the skirt and into whatever is your version of a great big cardboard box covered in scribbles about sports teams. That's a game you're in with a fighting chance.

Love, Hate and Your Marketing Personality

Our chief operating officer at Sonar6 was a guy named Pete Weaver — a feisty, driven, talented operator and one of the most commercial people I've ever met. I think we hired him mainly because he had gray hair and that felt like it was going to add some credibility, but almost instantly he just started making stuff happen. Pete is the personification of that counterintuitive truth "if you want something done, ask a busy person to do it." Watching Pete work is like watching an octopus juggle.

But Pete has one huge failing: He loves Bruce Springsteen. To the point of traveling the world to get his Boss on at multiple Springsteen shows a year. This is utterly unfathomable to me. I. Hate. Springsteen.

But guess what — Springsteen doesn't care. Bruce doesn't care about me hating his music at all. He doesn't care if my whole family and everyone on our street and all the people in our neighborhood hate him and his music. He doesn't need to care. Because Pete loves him enough to buy everything he's selling. Pete is one of Bruce Springsteen's *people*, and there are plenty enough Petes to support the Boss' whole career.

Early on at Sonar6 I made the mistake of caring about people who hated us. In fact, I worried about every person who didn't like us, and I *obsessed* over the people that hated us. And there seemed to be plenty. Even the tagline "At last, performance reviews that don't suck" had a huge number of detractors. People would write us emails that went something like this: "To whom it may concern, I was impressed with the functionality of your software but I would never buy it because of the offensive use of the word 'suck' in your marketing. How you would ever expect to build a business with such profanity is beyond me. Sincerely, Angry of Iowa."

My natural response was to try to placate the haters. I experimented with a more vanilla tagline: "At last, performance reviews that your staff will enjoy." Which offended no one (except for my own sensibilities), but also it appealed to no one. It wasn't memorable. It was a vaguely positive "meh." And "meh" has no place in marketing.

By removing the word "suck" from the tagline, I removed something important — the personality. Without "suck" it offended no one, but also it appealed to no one. *Marketing needs to have personality.*

Great marketers are like great conversationalists. Of course, marketing itself isn't a conversation — it's far too disjointed and one-way to be compared to a conversation. But great conversationalists and great marketers share a common goal: to engage their audience.

If you're at all like me, I'm sure you shy away from some people at parties. You groan inwardly as they approach, knowing they're unremittingly dull company. They're nice. They never offended you. But you don't want to talk to them because they lack personality.

Then there are those people who we seek out. We know they'll be entertaining, sometimes opinionated, often provocative. Always memorable. You leave the conversation richer for having had it. You might have learned something, been challenged, and you might even feel invigorated. Those people are conversationalists! They're full of personality.

In Chapter 1 we concluded that great marketing aims for

a human connection. If human connection is the ends, personality is the means.

At Sonar6 we developed a very consistent marketing personality. Look at that tagline again: "At last, performance reviews that don't suck." It was a great expression of our marketing personality. We were funny, in a slightly self-deprecating way (poking fun at the category that we chose to be in!). We were willing to upset the apple cart. And we called it as we saw it. Those three things were our marketing personality.

That big brown cardboard box wasn't just a stunt. It was also an expression of our marketing personality. Obviously funny (again, in a self-deprecating way), obviously disrupting the status quo, and more subtly calling it as we saw it — trade shows were not the best place to learn about online products.

Once we had our marketing personality established, everything else came very naturally. All the way from "I heart HR ladies" pens through to John being escorted off the show floor, these were all expressions of our marketing personality.

It was a big personality. And just like with partygoers, a big personality meant some people would love us and some people would hate us. And that is what it is. Trust me — Angry of Iowa was never going to buy our software anyway. She wasn't one of our people.

It's actually better to have 95 percent of people hating what you do and 5 percent of people loving it than to have 100 percent of people in a state of vaguely positive "meh." Because "vaguely positive meh" doesn't mean sales. The market is so full of choice that consumers seldom settle for something that's simply inoffensive. Even in an area as potentially dry as HR software, the secret to winning customers — our people, the people we were meant to be with — was to have personality.

Everyone Secretly Loves the Disrupter

When we started Sonar6 we were based in Auckland, but most of our growth ambitions — the customers and the funding that we wanted — were in California. We behaved like any business that starts in a small country or in a little city. We played down our New Zealand roots, trying instead to appear more Californian. Eventually we discovered that being from New Zealand was actually a huge help. It made us different. It helped get people's attention and it made us memorable. In a crowded market, getting someone's attention in the first place is a lot harder than later calming their fears about whether you really can deliver from New Zealand.

We were very careful about what aspects of being from New Zealand we emphasized. Our strongest theme was that being removed from the day-to-day world of U.S. business allowed us to think outside the box and be more inventive. This was true, a completely authentic statement about the company and what we thought set us apart. Things that were equally true, but that we didn't emphasize, included that our support team worked out of New Zealand and that our windows were plugged with boxes from inferior New Zealand-style pizza. In other words, we realized that we should be ourselves, but a carefully stage-managed version of ourselves. Marketing works best when it has a personality, and that personality only works if it's real.

One of the most enjoyable people in the world of HR that you could ever strike up a conversation with is Laurie Ruettimann. She's what my mother calls a firebrand. She's only 5 feet tall, but she's 10 feet tall, if you know what I mean. Starting as a blogger, then as a speaker on HR issues, then as a consultant to vendors in HR, she has built her position in the industry on a strong personality. Her original blog was called Punk Rock HR, and really that says it all. Any reader could immediately tell that she was disrupting the stuffy world of human resources. Some people probably hated her for that, but some people loved her — and that is, of course, the point.

The first time I ever talked to Laurie she looked up at me and said, confidently, "Everyone secretly loves the disrupter." She paused for a second, then said: "Actually, that may or may not be true, but it certainly helps your confidence if you believe it!"

Startup Marketing Hacks #8-11

8. Don't aim for vaguely positive.

Too many marketers waste their energy making sure that they don't do things that some people might dislike instead of focusing all their energy on doing things that some people — their people — will love.

9. Remember you're a marketer, not a doctor.

If you have to choose between memorable and professional, choose memorable.[4] You can explain how slick you are later.

10. Have personality (your own, but better).

Never pretend to be a version of someone else. You'll always be a shitty version. Be a carefully stage-managed version of yourself. Take the things that make your business different and amplify them. Turn these into your

---

[4] Unless you *are* a doctor. Then stunts are out.

marketing personality.

11. The Boss doesn't care about the haters.
The goal of marketing is to make people like you so much that they buy your stuff. They almost need to love you. If a side effect of making some people love you is that some people hate you, learn to not give a shit. They're just not your people. You're a startup; you can worry about the rest of the market later.

4.
Marketing Umami

The Sallies, Epsom, Auckland, Circa 1976

I grew up in Auckland. In those days the drive from the airport to town was a long wind through sleepy suburban streets, and if you were an Englishman making that slow trip, you couldn't help but be amused by the names of the Auckland suburbs that you would pass: Balmoral, Sandringham, Newmarket and Epsom (where I lived), all named after either British royal family castles or fancy racecourses.[5]

This isn't just a historical quirk. It's marketing.

Exactly how those suburbs got those names is conjecture and myth, but there must be a reason they ended up sounding so decidedly posh. The best guess is this: Most early European immigrants to New Zealand

---

[5] These places already had names, of course — indigenous Māori names, some of which survived the colonial renaming. But that's a whole other story.

were from Britain, so naming areas after places back home would be normal. The choice of names shows a distinct bias toward the fancy parts of the motherland. It seems folks wanted their areas to sound nice — desirable, even — so somewhere between unconscious bias and conscious design they chose the names of castles and racecourses and the like. After all, it's much more satisfying when sending a letter home to say you've settled in Sandringham rather than in Cabbage Tree Swamp. Desirability may well be the essence of marketing.

Epsom in 1976 had wide, flat streets lined with plane trees, weirdly stumpy from aggressive pruning by a council more worried about powerlines than aesthetics. California bungalows on quarter-acre sections lined the streets, and every second house had a friendly old lady with too many cats. In summer we never wore shoes, even when riding our bikes around the traffic-less roads looking for discarded glass soda bottles to return for the five-cent deposit, which was every balmy evening.

And every year, during the humid lead-up to the Southern Hemisphere Christmas, something magical happened in Epsom. Rumbling into my childhood utopia, on the back of a flatbed truck, was *the greatest piece of marketing I've ever seen.*

Do you have any childhood memories that are so glowing, so striking, that you need to check with your mother on whether they actually happened? That you didn't just dream them into your childhood recollections? I've checked with my Mum that this actually happened.

We would hear it first from a few blocks away: the distant low sound of the tubas. The occasional shrill note of the trumpeters. Like Radar from "M*A*S*H," my older brother would alert the household that "They're here again!" and we'd all rush out the front gate to wait, Mum and Dad rustling through the house for coins on the way out. Our neighbors would all start appearing along the street, exchanging Christmas pleasantries as the distant music became less distant, until the truck rolled around the corner and onto our street. And there it was, in all its majesty: *The greatest piece of marketing I've ever seen.*

Every year, the Salvation Army ran an appeal before Christmas to raise money for those who couldn't afford Christmas. And this is how they would do it: The Salvation Army brass band, a collection of old (to 6-year-old me) men dressed in striking red-and-black suits, would ride on a 10-ton flatbed truck, playing Christmas carols on their tubas and trumpets. No, really.

There was a banner on the side of the truck that read "Help the Poor." While the truck made its slow way up the street and the air filled with a mix of jaunty tunes and diesel fumes, the Salvation Army women (who seemed to be exclusively white-haired old ladies to 6-year-old me), also wearing striking red-and-black suits and hats, went door to door with collection buckets. Well, gate to gate actually, since everyone was already out on the street. We knew the drill. We had our coins ready.

Why is this *The greatest piece of marketing I've ever seen?* Because it's marketing that has stretched across the decades. I'm remembering the Salvation Army brass band in my street, from a period of my life where I can recall few of my friends and none of my teachers. Because it's marketing full of personality: It's old men in red suits playing trumpets. Because it's marketing that makes a human connection: Old ladies with buckets! Because its message was so clear: *Help the Poor.* You give money, people worse off than you get to have a better Christmas, and we, the hard-working folk walking your streets playing brass, we'll make sure that happens.

It wasn't slick. It wasn't thought up by the marketing department. In fact it probably wasn't even thought of as marketing. But it ticked all the boxes we've talked about that make marketing good. Human, clear, full of personality. Then somehow it transcended far beyond good marketing, into marketing gold. It had magic.

A Marketing Mystery

Marketing is full of dualities. For example, human connection is the high-water mark of startup marketing success, but getting there requires a strong marketing personality, and a strong marketing personality has the converse effect of turning some people off. I'm sure even in the Salvation Army example there were still plenty of curmudgeons, hiding in their houses behind closed blinds, mumbling unkind words, pretending they were out as the Sallies rolled down the street.

There's a certain yin and yang to it all. Many aspects of marketing are both contrary and complementary, none more so than the flipside of clarity: mystery. While clarity is critical to marketing success, marketing only ever reaches magical status when it balances that clarity with a measured dose of mystery.

Mystery is the umami of marketing. Umami is that mysterious fifth taste (alongside sweet, sour, bitter and salty) that translates from Japanese roughly as "pleasant savory taste." Mysterious in that its very existence has been argued over in Western culinary and scientific circles for nearly 100 years, but it is in fact an undeniable basic taste in cooking since Roman times.[6] The definitions of it always

---

[6] Romans used garum, a fermented fish sauce, to get that little bit of savory je ne sais quoi in their ancient pasta with red sauce.

seem to be filled with phrases like "difficult to describe" — hence, marketing umami.

One of our most successful early marketing programs at Sonar6 was an email titled "HR Black Swan Event." "HR" as in human resources, and "Black Swan Event" as in an event that comes as a surprise.[7]

The success of the campaign was based on getting lots of things right. I'll talk more about those shortly, but surprisingly one of the things that worked about that email subject line was the term "event." It turns out that a decent chunk of people opened it thinking that "event" referred to some kind of party, that maybe they were invited to, with "Black Swan" feeling close to black tie — but, well, more mysterious. It wasn't necessarily planned that way, but this ever-so-slightly tongue-tied piece of confusion really helped the campaign.

It's unsurprising, but people remember what they think about. One of the goals of your marketing, one of the ways to break through the marketing filter and be remembered, is to somehow force the audience to think, even for a second. Small elements of mystery are like unanswered questions. They remain in your audience's minds, helping break through the marketing filter and helping to increase memorability.

Cheesy in a Good Way. Like Fondue.

I remember trying to come to grips with the idea of mystery with Mark when the business was very new. We

---

[7] The term "Black Swan Event" comes from an ancient saying that used "black swan" as an example of something that did not exist, since everyone knew all swans were white. The saying lost its force after black swans were discovered in Australia.

wrote as part of our founding principles that we wanted a "sense of magic" in people's interactions with the company. In the spirit of marketing umami, what this meant was hard to describe. Eventually we settled on the idea of a pop-up book. From the outside the business looked like any other, but when you started to interact with us you would be immediately struck with the same wonder as when you open a pop-up book and a whole castle lifts up out of the page.

It's hard to say whether we ever really achieved this. Perhaps because mystery is so damn mysterious. Except that later I discovered that it isn't — mystery actually follows a pretty well-established set of rules. Sorry to disappoint you.

One of my favorite marketing examples for thinking about mystery is an insert that fell out of a golf magazine at my dentist's office one day in the late 1990s. The headline read "The secret I learned from the one-armed golfer." It was for a DVD series on improving your golf swing. Possibly a VHS box set. Regardless, the beauty of that line from a marketing perspective is that it piques the reader's interest so much that they want to find out more.[8]

There's an obvious element of mystery to it. It leaves the audience with a question. What is it about this golfer only having one arm that gives him or her some kind of advantage? What is the secret? But the reason that this is so effective goes beyond the straight element of mystery. This particular kind of mystery is actually a well-established trope.

A trope is a common (or overused) theme or device. It's

---

[8] A word of warning: While the one-armed golfer is still one of my all time favorites, this headline might be too much like clickbait to work now. I'll talk more about that in the next chapter.

often applied to the movies or TV, where the same kind of plot devices are used over and over again. The one-armed golfer is an example of what TVTropes.org (yes, there is a website for everything) refers to as the Disability Superpower. A character is born with, or acquires, some handicap that prevents him or her from functioning normally. However, he or she then develops something that not only makes up for what's missing, but goes beyond it. We see this in the movie "Forrest Gump." When Forrest breaks out of the leg braces that he has been made to wear as a child, he can suddenly run as fast as the wind. There's a whole subcategory of this trope just related to blindness: Blind musicians, having lost their sight, gain greater musical ability. Basically there is this strongly understood idea in fiction (and in popular culture) that disability in one area creates strength in another.

So when we read "the secret I learned from the one-armed golfer," our mind is already trained to go for the trope. Most people, at least subconsciously, will make this sort of connection. "Because he only has one arm, he must have had to overcome that somehow, and so that handicap has actually given him an advantage. At golf."

Why are tropes so common in TV and movies? Why are the same themes repeated over and over? Because they're part of the cultural background, so they're easy to digest and they're comfortably familiar and, therefore, likeable. That's gold in the short-attention-span world of TV and movies. And attention spans are even shorter in marketing.

For mystery to work in marketing, the audience needs to expect the secret. By playing into established tropes, marketing can achieve the magic of mystery within a really short attention span. Mystery is about leaving the audience with a question. Tropes are about ensuring the answer is within easy grasp.

If you search for "tropes" online, you'll find a whole raft of concepts that are generally understood as part of our popular culture, but are never explicitly stated. "Forrest Gump" is a treasure trove of tropes. Forrest is an idiot Houdini: functionally developmentally disabled, yet all his decisions lead to success, wealth and fame. He even buys stock in a fledgling Apple Inc., believing it's "some kind of fruit company." To quote TVTropes.org: "Forrest is so dense that he routinely attempts things other people wouldn't even consider, and so single-minded that he puts his maximum effort into everything he does. As a result, he meets spectacular success while the skeptics are left scratching their heads."

This idea of being born lucky is a well-established trope. We expect Homer Simpson's actions, however idiotic, to never lead to actual harm. At the other end of the spectrum we expect James Bond to escape, brilliantly, even when the odds are stacked against him. Forrest, Bond, Homer: They were all Born Lucky.

This same trope is used in marketing. The Most Interesting Man In The World is an ad campaign for Dos Equis beer. It features a distinguished older gentleman, who, like a classier version of Chuck Norris, seems to be capable of many extraordinary things:

"He once taught a dog to bark … in Spanish."

"He once parallel parked a train."

"He's a lover not a fighter, but he's also a fighter, so don't get any ideas." (That's my favorite.)

The campaign absolutely drips mystery, but the mystery is digestible; it plays into the Born Lucky trope.

We didn't consciously start building trope-based campaigns at Sonar6. Rather, we just realized one day that the campaigns that worked best were the ones that utilized tropes. Mystery was a big part of the success of our Black

Swan Event campaign. The body copy read like this:

*There has been a Black Swan Event. Out of a lab in New Zealand (of all places) comes a very simple idea that changes the annual performance review (clue: it's about making them **useful!**).*

This plays into a well-worn trope: Revolutionary ideas come from unexpected places. Of course, like many tropes, there's a factual basis to this idea. But the trope dramatically overplays it, as does the body copy above. And it works. Digestible mystery.

Romance and Other Emotions

When I was 19 I was in a plane crash.

My friend Don MacKenzie had his private pilot's license. He had entered a vintage plane rally in a borrowed Piper Cub. The Cub is a cult plane — a bright yellow fabric-over-metal two-seater from the 1930s with just enough engineering to keep it in the air, and no more. For example, the fuel gauge is a cork that floats in the fuel tank and that's attached to a wire that sticks up through the fuel cap. As the fuel goes down in the tank, the cork sinks and the wire dips down. To ascertain range the pilot looks out the window and judges the length of the piece of wire.

Anyway, while flying over one of the most remote pieces of the New Zealand coastline, the Piper Cub ceased to work. The engine seized. I remember first being struck by how quiet it suddenly became. Small planes are loud, but with the engine off and the propeller just sitting upright and motionless, they're eerily quiet. I was then struck by how engineless planes don't really glide. They just lose altitude and head toward the sea.

Don expertly ditched the plane. He really did. We didn't cartwheel. We just came to an abrupt stop in the ocean. So we sat in the plane on the surface of the water for a bit, chatting. It was surreal.

We opened the door before we ditched, as is normal practice (things you learn), and after a short while a wave came along that flooded the cockpit, so the plane abruptly sank to the level of its overhead wing. I got the life jackets and we got out, reconvening on the roof. We sat up there for a bit, and we might have even talked about rescue, but the plane sank further and we eventually found ourselves standing on the wings with just our heads poking out of the water.

So we swam. Arms linked. On our backs, in the relentless New Zealand summer sun. Land seemed a distance away, and, discouragingly, for most of the 90 minutes we were swimming it didn't seemed to get any closer. On later inspection it seems that while we ditched about 1.5 kilometers (about a mile) from shore, we managed to swim 6 kilometers (about 3 miles) because of the current. When we did finally get close to land, our wash of relief quickly turned to panic as we realized that landfall was cliffs, kelp and fierce waves.

Eventually, in a story far too complex for this text, we were rescued — and I will, of course, be forever grateful for the wonderful people who made that possible (and to Don for his level-headedness). My Mum is also grateful, which is a nice segue into what happened next. I became famous for about 15 minutes, during which time I completely forgot I even had a mother. It was heady, I tell you.

The rescue helicopter took us to the nearest town, Kaitaia, in the far north of New Zealand. By the time we got there, news of the two 19-year-olds and their big swim had spread. This was a big deal. It felt like the whole town had come out to welcome us. Don and I got out of the chopper in our borrowed clothes (never swim in jeans) to the rapturous applause of about 200 people. I felt like Lindbergh, just a bit more sunburned.

A lady from the airfield told me I could have anything I wanted from the cafeteria, gratis. Nineteen-year-old me was over the moon. Proper rock-star treatment! I can even remember what I had, making my way gleefully around the self-service cabinets: a meat pie, a grated cheese and grated carrot sandwich on white bread, and something that we used to refer to as a "fly cemetery," which is a sort of raisin-based slice that I'll just leave to describe itself. This. Was. Fame.

As I stuffed my face someone asked me if I'd been put off flying, and I joked "No, but I've been put off swimming." Fifty people laughed, and 50 more leaned in and said "what did he say?" Soon everyone was laughing, and I was adored.

After 15 minutes of eating and shaking hands and answering questions, someone asked "What did your mother say when you told her?" and I suddenly remembered I had a mother. Someone arranged a phone call, and when I rang her she was crying. Mainly because the radio had reported that a plane had ditched in the ocean and my mother had made the instinctive link that the two men referred to — "breaking news, two men have crashed a plane into the sea near North Cape and are now fighting for their lives in shark-infested waters, now back to the hits" — were Don and me. What the radio neglected to do was to report that we had been rescued, so she didn't know we were safe until I rang. Including cafeteria time, hours had passed.

My adoring Kaitaia public slowly dispersed and I made my way back to Auckland with Don. We were on the six o'clock news and in the papers, and the plane crash generally made my life better. I was suddenly more popular.

Particularly in bars. I was the beneficiary of the romance of being a plane-crash survivor.

Let me explain. Stories of leather-clad barnstormers, ace fighter pilots and jungle plane-crash survivors are part of the backdrop of our storytelling culture. Even now, decades later, when I tell the story of the crash I'm immediately positioned as part adventurer, part daredevil, part brave, resourceful soul. That's what "plane-crash survivor" evokes.

When I say the *romance of a plane-crash survivor*, I'm not using romance as in romantic love, but rather as in the *romance of travel*, or *the romance of Paris*. Some things occupy a different part of our collective imagination than others. Some things are almost always viewed with a pleasant nostalgia. They evoke a pleasant emotion, and emotion cuts through the marketing filter. You knew this was eventually going to come back to marketing, right?

Smart marketing plays into emotional cues. The emotion doesn't have to be romance, or even to be positive, to have a similar effect. Hope, joy, loss — these are all emotions used in marketing.

One of the clothing lines of Benetton Group is The United Colors of Benetton. The brand name itself has strong emotional cues. While the meaning isn't immediately clear, it tells a story of inclusion and joy. In a handful of words, it conjures up a brave new world, devoid of racism, embracing multiculturalism, and it miraculously makes that relevant to apparel.

When Benetton ties that mysterious brand name to emotionally powerful imagery, the story expands and the magic grows. In the early 1990s Benetton ran an ad for The United Colors of Benetton picturing young AIDS activist David Kirby dying in a hospital bed, surrounded by family. The emotions of loss, acceptance and love were writ large.

The beauty of emotional cues is that, just like a little bit of mystery, they make the brain think. If the brain is thinking, it's engaged, and that's the biggest challenge of marketing. Indeed, the mechanism may even be simpler. Emotional cues make people feel, and feeling is memorable.

If I tell someone I was in a plane crash, they have an emotional reaction. Their brain kicks in. They formulate questions in their head, then they answer some of those questions themselves. Basically they're stimulated to think. The outcome: memorability. Useful when you're 19.

Stories of the Psychologically Privileged

There's something else about the plane-crash story that made it great marketing for 19-year-old Mike: Simply, it's a *story*.

Cognitive scientist Daniel T. Willingham summarizes it beautifully in his paper "The Privileged Status of Story":

Everybody loves a good story. Even small children who have difficulty focusing in class will sit with rapt attention in the presence of a good storyteller. But stories are not just fun. There are important cognitive consequences of the story format. Psychologists have therefore referred to stories as "psychologically privileged," meaning that our minds treat stories differently than other types of material. People find stories interesting, easy to understand, and easy to remember.

He goes on to explain the nature of good storytelling, of how professional writers follow the four C's[9]:

- *Causality.* Events in stories initiate other events. *The plane*

---

[9] Amusingly, if you search the internet for the "4C's of storytelling," you can find dozens of different combinations of four words beginning with C that define good stories. Storytelling may well be more of an art than a science.

engine stopped, so we crashed in the sea.
- *Conflict.* Obstacles prevent a central character from meeting their goals. *The plane sank so we had to swim.*
- *Complications.* The character's efforts to remove the obstacle create complications. *When we finally reached the landfall it was cliff, kelp and fierce waves.*
- *Character.* Interesting characters are observed in action. *I survived a plane crash! But I also forgot to call my mother.*

Every piece of good marketing is effectively a story. And most of the time they're short — often very, very short. A 90-second website video works best if it tells a story, but so does a tagline or even a logo. As a marketer it's worth honing your storytelling skills, and it's particularly worth trying to do so in the most concise way possible.

I love finding examples of concise storytelling. "Levi Stubbs' Tears" is a song by the loquacious English singer-songwriter Billy Bragg. The opening verse is a story in itself: *With the money from her accident she bought herself a mobile home. So at least she could get some enjoyment out of being alone.*

Think about this in terms of the four C's. Causality: There has been an accident that leads to the purchase of a mobile home. Conflict: She is going to be alone. Complications: The "at least" implies complication, a hint of the struggle to enjoy life after a traumatic event. Character: A rich character is described through her actions. She's a fighter, she's an optimist, she's in search of some adventure, despite a loss.

All of this in 24 words. Thanks, Billy.

The United Colors of Benetton and the picture of David Kirby is still-fewer words, paired with powerful image. It also fulfills the requirements of compelling story.

Even our Sonar6 tagline, "At last, performance reviews that don't suck," hints at elements of the four C's. The "at last" at the start gives a sense of conflict, complications and causality. It implies that there's been a long time during which performance reviews have sucked; that there has probably been a search, or even a quest, to make them better; and that now, at last, the suckiness has gone. Without the "at last" it would be lifeless. Standing alone, "performance reviews that don't suck" isn't a story.

Logos are the shortest story of them all. So concise that they'll always struggle to fulfill the four C's, although some manage to transcend that limitation. The silvery white Apple logo still manages to capture some action. After all, someone must have taken that singular bite out of it. Whether it's a symbolic forbidden fruit (a trope!) or just the start of a fruit snack, there's a thread of causation.

The Sea Shepherd Conservation Society is a marine conservation organization that uses aggressive direct-action tactics to protect dolphins (more dolphins!) and whales from slaughter. The Sea Shepherd flag, with its skull, trident and shepherd's crook arranged in the shape of a Jolly Roger, tells a concise story, replete with causality, conflict and character.

Basically, anything that helps turn your marketing into a story makes a huge difference. Because being a story gives privileged status. Stories can break through the marketing filter and be remembered.

One more thing from Willingham about stories:

The reason that stories are engaging may be inherent in their structure. Story structure naturally leads the listener (or reader) to make inferences that are neither terribly easy, nor impossibly difficult. New information that is a little bit puzzling, but which we can understand, is deemed more interesting than new information that is either very easy or very difficult to understand. For example, people enjoy working crossword puzzles, anagrams, and the like, but only if they are moderately difficult. They are tedious if too easy, and frustrating if too hard.

This circles right back to the yin-yang of balancing clarity with mystery. If your content is 100 percent clear but 100 percent without mystery, it may still work, but it'll engage the audience less. If it's too mysterious it'll frustrate the audience and have limited engagement. Mystery needs to be in the middle. Marketing needs to be just a little bit puzzling.

In the short-attention-span world of marketing, how do you reach that balance? How do you insert digestible mystery? By using tropes, emotional cues and storytelling structure.

Postscript: The Prestige

So now I've talked about the techniques for giving your marketing a measured dose of mystery to increase engagement. But I started this chapter talking about the magic of the Sallies on my childhood street, and I want to take the magic metaphor to its logical conclusion: the design of a magic trick. What follows is not a formula.

The movie "The Prestige" is a beautiful Victorian period piece, with stars including the late, great David Bowie as Nikola Tesla (a lovely combination of two of my favorites), that tells the story of a rivalry between two magicians. There's a scene where a character goes to some lengths to explain how a magic trick is constructed in three parts, and I can't do that better than by quoting. You can do this in Michael Caine's voice if you'd like:

Every great magic trick consists of three parts or acts. The first part is called "The Pledge." The magician shows you something ordinary: a deck of cards, a bird or a man. He shows you this object. Perhaps he asks you to inspect it to see if it is indeed real, unaltered, normal. But of course ... it probably isn't. The second act is called

"The Turn." *The magician takes the ordinary something and makes it do something extraordinary. Now you're looking for the secret ... but you won't find it, because of course you're not really looking. You don't really want to know. You want to be fooled. But you wouldn't clap yet. Because making something disappear isn't enough; you have to bring it back. That's why every magic trick has a third act, the hardest part, the part we call "The Prestige."*

The first time I ever got an Uber was outside McCormick Place in Chicago. McCormick Place is a behemoth among convention centers, with acres of polished marble, glass and steel. The HR Tech conference had just finished and thousands of HR people were spilling out of the convention center. It was cold in that bone-chilling way that Chicago specializes in.

There was a huge line for taxis and only sporadic taxis. The line was not moving. My breath was forming a cold cloud in front of my face. I was rocking from side to side, trying to stay warm. We all were. I'm sure everyone was thinking the same thing that I was: Go inside and stay warm and lose my place in line, or stay out here for an indefinite amount of time and freeze.

Then, as I was pondering, a black car pulled up adjacent to the line, and a guy sauntered out of the convention center, got straight into it and was whisked away. Huh? Then the same scene was repeated. Again and again before it dawned on me: Uber! Sure, I'd heard of it, but up to this point I had never really had a problem with just hailing a cab.

So I went back into the warmth of the foyer and downloaded Uber on my phone. I remember being weirdly underwhelmed by what I guess was a pretty early version of the interface. But "The Pledge" was obvious. Within a few minutes of becoming an Uber customer I could see a driver (with his name and picture!) driving toward me on a map on my phone, and he was due there in 12 minutes. Sure, 12 minutes is kind of slow, but hey, I wasn't waiting in a freezing taxi line any more. Outside, it began to sleet.

Great days are a collection of small pleasures. When my black car arrived, I couldn't really hide my joy. With a deliberate jauntiness, a swagger even, I swung through the door onto the forecourt. I let the full force of the sleet hit me in the face, embraced it, knowing that it was only footsteps to my waiting car. As the driver and I greeted each other by name, "The Turn" was complete. It was a small piece of magic, enough to satisfy one tired marketer.

Sitting in the back seat, I started to fiddle with the app. I was surprised at how little human language was used; I can see now how deliberate that is. Consumers recognize utility instantly; there's no need to happy-talk them. Clarity and convenience are closely tied. And a car with a driver, that's a very human thing anyway.

We ground through slow traffic. The driver and I chatted about Chicago's failed bid to host the Olympics, about steak, about blues. Then we talked about Uber, about how I got to rate my driver after the trip, and he got to rate me as a customer. My God, Chicago can be bleak at the start of winter, but the warmth of the people more than compensates. There was some grumbling about road construction. Eventually we got to my destination. And then: "The Prestige."

I got out of the car. I said goodbye. I walked away.

I didn't fiddle with change. I didn't try to work out what I was supposed to tip. I didn't argue with the driver about why, despite the Visa sticker on the side of the car, he wouldn't accept my credit card. I didn't try to jam my change back in my wallet while other drivers were laying on their horns. I didn't have to do any of the things that I had never really realized were shitty about leaving a cab until I didn't have to do them anymore.

I felt somewhere between being just dropped off by a friend and being Kanye arriving at a premiere. Probably closer to the former, but either way, that feeling right there, that was The Prestige. The third act.

You might ask, is the Uber experience even marketing? Isn't it a product experience? But I'd counter that it's almost all of Uber's marketing. In one ride I was a fan, and that's the essence of good marketing. The personality, the human parts of the experience, are implicit in a car with a driver (especially with two-way ratings). The clarity across the whole experience was exceptional. But the thing that really made me an instant convert was the subtle magic of the whole experience.

Startup Marketing Hacks #12-14

12. Use a little mystery to make people think.

There's a yin-yang to marketing. Good marketing starts with clarity. But great marketing balances clarity with a measured dose of mystery. The mystery forces the audience to think, and people remember what they think about. Being remembered is an important goal in itself. Whenever you're constructing a campaign or activity, ask yourself "Will people still be thinking about this tomorrow?"

13. The secret I learned from the one-armed golfer.

Adding mystery is surprisingly formulaic. To suit the attention span of marketing, mystery works like this: It should make the audience ask a question, with an answer that is within easy grasp.

Three techniques:

- *Reference tropes.* Tropes are common themes in fiction or popular culture. At Sonar6 we played on the trope that

"revolutionary ideas come from unexpected places," a concept so well accepted that we never needed to explain it.
- *Use emotional cues.* Common emotions, like romance, hope or loss, also let you significantly condense communication, because consumers can feel their way into a connection.
- *Use story structure.* Stories are psychologically privileged. From the complexity within a 90-second website video down to something as concise as a logo, if your marketing tells stories it will encourage people to make inferences.

14. Never over-season the broth.

New information that's a little bit puzzling but that we can understand with a little effort is more interesting than new information that's either very easy or very difficult to understand.

If your content is absolutely clear but without mystery, it may still work, but it will engage the audience less. If it's too mysterious it will frustrate the audience, limiting connection. Mystery needs to be in the middle. Your marketing needs to be just a little bit of a puzzle.[10]

---

[10] Like other basic tastes, umami is pleasant only within a relatively narrow concentration range.

5.
Ladies and Gentlemen!

Throw Stuff at John!

When I arrived at the office parking lot that morning, preparations were already well underway. There was a selection of big water guns and some buckets of water. The firehose was laid out. There were baskets filled with balls: tennis balls (normal and giant-sized), all sorts of beach balls and some soccer balls. Lined up behind were bigger objects: Swiss exercise balls and moon-hopper toys.

This was Kai's idea. We were coming to the end of the year, our fourth year in, and the sales numbers weren't at target. So we'd do an end-of-year special. Like we were a car dealership! And we'd promote it with this video where John, the CEO, would hold a small whiteboard with a discount percentage written on it while the rest of the Sonar6 team threw all sorts of stuff at him. We'd keep throwing stuff at him until he wrote down a discount we were satisfied with.

A straightforward plan: Throw stuff at John.

Kai was in the foyer mixing up big buckets of colored goop: water and flour mixed with food coloring, in our corporate colors (we were always on brand). These were for the finale. John was outside in his nice Sonar6 branded T-shirt and smart jeans, *startup stylez*. Breathing deeply. Doing a few quick jumps. Shaking his hands. Hyping himself up. All proper startup folk know that you do what it takes.

The shoot started with John holding his sign and us squirting him with water. He looked more and more unhappy as he got thoroughly drenched. But the team was enjoying this. I was enjoying this!

Next we started throwing the tennis balls, hundreds of them. The shot looked great. Then someone hurled a moon-hopper at John. It caught him off-balance and he tumbled backward into the roller door. But John's a trouper, and since it was all planned as a single shot no one wanted to break continuity to check whether he was OK.

The shoot progressed and John got slammed with larger and larger items. There was a set of stairs that ran up to the entrance to our building, and I was standing at the top holding one of the buckets of goop, the sky blue one, so that as the final act I could throw the contents from a height onto John's head. The shoot had descended into utter chaos. John had the firehose on him, there were still balls being thrown at him and he was reeling from having gone backward into the roller door, but like a pro he was on script, wiping down the whiteboard, writing ever larger discounts.

Ten percent, 15 percent, 20 percent … 20 percent was our signal to go for the finale.

Kai threw the purple goop first. The buckets of goop were heavy so it was awkward to throw them, and his shot came up short, with purple goop landing mainly on John's jeans. As John looked down someone hurled one of the oversized tennis balls and it hit him clean in the side of the head. Dom chucked the green goop, which made better contact, hitting John at chest height. I knew that for real visual impact I was going to have to go for a full body hit. So I leaned right out and with all my strength hurled the contents of my bucket onto John's head.

The heavy, gluey contents of the bucket somehow seemed to pull the bucket with them, and instead of just throwing the contents I ended up throwing the bucket as well. My aim was good. The bucket and about 50 pounds of flour, water and food coloring nearly knocked John to the ground. Nothing ever goes exactly to plan.

Kai, thinking fast and focused on continuity, decided to throw the other empty buckets as well. We were all in hysterics as John finally wrote 25 percent on his whiteboard. He stood there holding the sign, wet, forlorn and covered in colored goop. That frame went onto to become the main image of the whole campaign.

The end-of-year promotion was a huge success, our biggest yet. We used the video in our marketing to our opt-in lists. Prospects talked about it, even shared it. It stimulated people who were considering buying but who hadn't had a compelling reason to actually get over the line. Our end-of-year sale worked!

Later, when we did a debrief on the campaign, we tried to understand what made it more successful than previous campaigns. We decided it was just good content. A very easy-to-understand message, delivered in an irreverent way, had both cut through the noise in the marketplace and connected with prospects in a human way. Throwing stuff at the boss. Simply perfect. Case closed.

But — and this is an important *but* — looking back on it now, in all the back-slapping on great content, we missed the most fundamental reason that the "throw stuff at John" promotion was our most successful. It was largely a hit because, four years in, we finally had a big enough audience that if we did some great marketing we had some people to market to!

I'll say it again. *We had an audience.* It's one thing to make great marketing content, but if you have no one to share it with, no one who's willing to read your email or watch your video, then it's worth nothing. When we wanted to stimulate sales before year-end, we actually had an audience of people to market to.

When I used to do marketing in an established corporation, I never thought about audience. People wanted to watch our stuff, and if they didn't want to we'd still just ram it down their throats. We could afford to market broadly, because our target market was basically everyone.

But startups are far too small to talk to everyone. A startup has to build a group of interested people, then talk to them. So the first goal of marketing in a startup is to build an audience.

The One-Two Punch

My first conversation with Ian Goldsmith was over the phone. He began by speaking very thoughtfully, calmly explaining in a posh English accent how he could help build up our sales leads. As the discussion carried on he got more and more animated, working himself up into a into a high-speed, excited patter, like an East London barrow-boy selling knockoff watches. I got off the phone, impressed but a little baffled. I couldn't really place him, and now, years later, I still don't exactly know where he's from or what his background is. I've had meetings with him in cafés in several countries, and was never quite sure whether he was a visitor or a local. He's an enigma.

But he's an enigma who knows more about audience building than anyone else I've met. Ian is the mad scientist of audience building. He has probably challenged my thinking on marketing more than anyone else. Most importantly he taught me the simple Equation of Audience Building:

Excited New People Joining Audience > Disinterested People Leaving Audience

Basically, you need to add people to your audience faster than you lose them, otherwise you'll never succeed. The great audience-builders are those marketers who do a great job of adding people to their audience *and* a great job of keeping people in their audience.[11]

Under Ian's guidance we developed a simple two-step approach to marketing: (1) build an audience and (2) market to that audience. The one-two punch.

Content Marketing: Is That Uncool Yet?

When Ian started working with Sonar6, he hit everything with such gusto that I just let him run, prepared to either bask in the collective glory or help pick up the pieces.

Ian understood the dark arts of list building and list trading.[12] One day he broke our support ticketing service

---

[11] In marketing, an audience is "a group of people you communicate with." A loose definition of your audience might be "people who see your print ads," but a more rigorous and useful way to think about your audience in a startup is people who have, in some way, agreed to receive communications from you — for example, by opting-in to receiving your emails or liking you on Facebook.

[12] List trading is the rather dubious practice of taking your existing list of

by using it to send thousands of unsolicited emails, but the effort garnered us more than 100 new audience members. Another time I woke up to find a cease-and-desist message from the office of Jack Welch, former CEO of General Electric, in my inbox. Ian had implied in an email that Jack Welch endorsed Sonar6, which wasn't *exactly* true. Actually it wasn't even *slightly* true. But hey, that stuff is collateral damage. The guy was a genius.

Building an audience isn't just about getting people's email addresses or Facebook likes; it's about making people actively interested in and excited about the communication they're getting from you. Ian gave us a bit of a head start. He was masterful at understanding aspects of popular culture that got people's attention. When gamification of everything was hot, Sonar6 was all about gamification. When the black swan concept was being written about, it was Ian who introduced it into our marketing.

What Ian was teaching us was content marketing. The goal of content marketing is not to pimp your product or lay on the hard sell. Rather the aim is to build your audience by offering them content that they find engaging and educational. Later, once they're engaged, you're in a good position to offer your product to already-interested potential buyers. Content marketing is a big part of step one in the one-two punch. It's one of the best ways for a startup to build that essential audience. Content marketing, however, has fashions. Let me expand.

The content in content marketing can take a range of forms. When we started our audience-building strategy,

---

customers' or potential customers' email addresses and trading those with a third party for their list, effectively doubling the size of your list. This is then often repeated. It's bottom-feeding activity of marginal legality in many jurisdictions. It's also pretty common and effective.

"thought leadership" was all the rage and a key part of the content marketing arsenal. What is thought leadership? Like all buzzwords, it has been so broadly applied that the precise meaning has become unclear. The internet tells me that thought leaders are "the informed opinion leaders and the go-to people in their field of expertise."

Genuine thought leadership is indeed a pretty great marketing approach. For example, when automated marketing was new, I came across an e-book by a company called Marketo explaining how drip marketing worked.[13] It was a godsend, an instructional booklet in a new field, and, at the time, many marketers referenced this document. I think I was vaguely aware that Marketo also made marketing automation software, but that was beside the point. In the field of automated marketing, Marketo was the go-to place to find out what you needed to know. When the time came to buy a marketing automation system at Sonar6, Marketo was our preferred vendor. We trusted them to tell us what we needed to buy, which was, unsurprisingly, their own product.

However, as you know if you've ever attended a plodding lecture about a topic you're not interested in — or even just sat through an in-flight safety video — educational material in and of itself is not necessarily compelling. In fact, there are two big risks associated with using a thought-leader-type content strategy. First, your market may not be as hungry for education as you think. I think we were lucky in the early days with Sonar6. There was a bit of a dearth of material on HR and people did seem to be engaged by our educational content, but this

---

[13] Drip marketing is the concept of feeding your potential customers information about your product over time in small, easily digestible pieces. It's often used by businesses selling complex B2B products.

will not always be the case. No matter how important your specialist field is to you, it's unlikely to be as important to the market. So the first risk is that people are bored by your useful educational content, because it just doesn't hit the mark with them.

The second risk is probably worse. It's easy for educational content to become not just boring, but actively annoying. Think about it like this — random guy from random tiny startup starts sending you "useful educational material" on a field you've been working in for 25 years. Who died and made him the guru of HR (or whatever it is you're talking about)? The risk is that your carefully thought-out educational content comes off as condescending, earnest and grating. If bad thought leadership were a person, he'd have no friends.

The right way to work your content marketing is to make it also follow the tricks we've been talking about to break through people's marketing filters: human, clear, personality-driven, perhaps even slightly mysterious.

Remember the ad for the golf-coaching videos from the last chapter, "The secret I learned from a one-armed golfer"? That headline almost forces you to read more. It's human, clear and has personality and mystery. And it promises education. But here's where you need to be careful, because while this content ticks the boxes I've laid out in the past couple of chapters, it also suffers from being "funny and unexpected," which used to be a good thing but now sort of isn't. The problem is that everyone has gotten on the "funny and unexpected" bandwagon. In fact, this kind of content marketing has become an industry in itself. "This girl started singing on the street. You won't believe what happened next!" "20 annoying things that hubbies do; number 7 is so true!" "What Marcia Brady Looks Like Now Is Jaw-Dropping!"

In the years since I admired that golfing ad, a bigger effect has come into play. "Funny and unexpected" content looks like marketing now. Remember the discussion about how we literally don't see marketing? That's the problem with "funny and unexpected" content marketing today. People's marketing filters are all over it. As always happens, marketing ruined itself.

Are you confused? Is content marketing cool or uncool now? Well, if it's good, it's great, and it will help you build that essential audience. But if it's bad, it's really bad.

So how do you make sure your content marketing is genuinely engaging, and not dumb, annoying, patronizing or just screened out by the marketing filter? For Sonar6 it turned out that part of the answer was to go dancing.

Dancing HR Ladies Take Atlanta

"Who wants to go dancing!" It wasn't a question; it was a call to action. I was at the bar at HREvolution, a chaotic un-conference full of HR folks discussing bleeding-edge HR. It had been a long but utterly fascinating day, and now, apparently, we were all going dancing.

Human resources has its own strong identity. I remember, soon after we started Sonar6, being asked by a reporter whether I had been an HR person, to which I replied "No, but I have been a victim of HR." The stereotypical HR department consists of middle-aged women with Coach handbags, who wear capri pants with pantyhose, own several cats each and occasionally storm in on their broomsticks to kill whatever joy exists in the modern workplace. There are more women than men in HR, and the Coach handbag thing is universally true, but the rest of it … well, like all stereotypes it's at right angles to the truth. The men and women at HREvolution were energized forward-thinkers, more stimulating company than you'd find at many business events. And they weren't unusual for HR.

"Techno or hip-hop?" someone asked. Coming from New Zealand, this was a question I hadn't previously thought of. More than one kind of dancing? Who knew? We were in Atlanta, and downtown is apparently a hotbed of hip-hop clubs, so that was the choice. Before long about 20 of us descended on some random club. It was quite early in the night, and we were all good-natured about going through the metal detector and being frisked. Coach handbags were carefully checked for concealed handguns. I imagine the club's staff was a little bemused at this group of mainly older women in smart navy outfits jiving in a tight circle on the dance floor, but the drinks flowed and we partied hard.

The DJ was phenomenal, the sound system was thumping, and I'm sure my companions were shouting inappropriate personnel jokes at each other, as HR people are prone to do after a few drinks. I, however, was getting kind of distracted by the rest of the crowd now filling the club. It was starting to look a lot like the video for Tupac's "California Love," but with a gaggle of HR ladies front and center. I'm sure mentioning Tupac Shakur in Atlanta is in itself some kind of terrible East Coast-West Coast hip-hop faux pas. Let's just say I felt like I didn't really understand the rules, and I wasn't sure if we were welcome.

I vaguely suggested to a few of the ladies that perhaps we should move on, but one thing that HR folk are very good at is ignoring stereotypes and preconceptions. And, after all, no one had guns, we knew that much. So we stayed, partying late into the night. Some of the club-goers looked at us strangely, but most just ignored us. In the end the most eventful happening at the club was someone (*not* an HR lady) sitting on my lap and attempting to feed me a slice of cake.

When we did finally step outside to go home, it all got a bit urban. There were sirens and cop cars and people thrown up against the alleyway wall with their arms in the air. There were a couple of guys sitting on the curb in handcuffs. Hundreds of people were milling around, looking tense. Pushing through this melee came the gaggle of HR ladies and me. One of the ladies asked where we might find cabs, only to be told that cabs don't come to that part of Atlanta in the early hours of a Sunday morning. They'll drop you off at 10 p.m., but they won't be coming back to pick you up when you're done. So we started the long walk back to the conference hotel.

After a few blocks, the air felt less heavy and we all began to relax and laugh about what a great night it had been. What I came to realize there in Atlanta was that HR really is a tribe. It has its own normal, its own way of behaving, its own way of speaking, its own version of a great night out. And they — the HR folk, the jiving ladies, my companions — were all totally comfortable with that. To an outside observer our circle looked out of place in that club, but the HR ladies' confidence in their shared tribe carried them through.

The problem with this, as I realized walking back through the mean streets of Atlanta, is that I wasn't part of that tribe. I was a tech guy from New Zealand, and the people I wanted to sell our product to were mostly HR women from corporate America. How I thought about the world and how they thought about the world wasn't the same. The things that I thought everyone took for granted were probably just the things that other tech guys in New Zealand took for granted. In other words, my inner marketer noted, "I don't think like these people." I wasn't part of my audience — yet.

You HR, Me Jane Goodall

One of my favorite tech success stories is GitHub. GitHub falls into the rather arcane category of developer tools. It's a cloud-based code repository and version-control system. The tool lets multiple contributors work on the same piece of software without losing track of the changes or stepping on one another's progress. These sort of tools existed long before GitHub, but GitHub's success lay in making those tools better, and getting everyone to use their version. In a few years GitHub has gone from an idea thought up by a handful of coders to being a basic requirement for any team developing software.

There's a whole GitHub mythology online about how it achieved this ubiquity, but the best summary of its early marketing strategy that I've heard, from when it was just starting up in the Bay Area, is this: "Make sure that at every single developer meetup in the area at least one person is wearing a GitHub hoodie."

The more you learn about GitHub, the more you realize that so much of its success has been driven by being involved in events and discussions with developers — its audience, the tribe who uses its products. Today, with millions of users around the world, it still primarily goes to market by sponsoring and hosting developer events, and ensuring that there are people there in their GitHub hoodies, talking about how useful GitHub is.

The GitHub people are part of the tribe of developers. They influence that crowd from within, and in turn their offerings are influenced by what they learn from the tribe they're part of. The GitHub person in the hoodie is marketing, but she or he is hopefully not dry, not boring and doesn't get filtered out. This model is fantastic if you can make it work.

There is, however, a really big difference between GitHub selling to coders and Sonar6 selling to HR people. GitHub people were coders themselves. They were natives. At Sonar6 we were not native HR speakers. We had to first learn the language and assimilate to the group. To get really serious about audience building, we needed to become part of the HR tribe. We needed to start to talk like HR people, think like HR people and dance like HR people.

Soon after my Atlanta dancing epiphany, we started making a very conscious effort to get closer to our audience. We began following HR blogs, commenting and getting involved in the conversation. We joined HR groups on LinkedIn. We started talking much more deeply to our customers, and not just about our product. We went to the HR events our customers recommended. I ended up with hundreds of HR friends on my own Facebook friends list. And, over time, what started as a cold-blooded strategy to do anything we could think of to get closer to HR morphed into effortless, joyous inclusion in the HR tribe.

Becoming like our customers transformed the way we talked. We developed an HR sense of humor. In our communications with our audience we'd make fun of ourselves as if we were HR people, and we were so in tune that most of the time we'd get away with it.

As well as deeply understanding our audience (and therefore being able to tailor our content for them), we also became connected to HR influencers: people who'd been around much longer than we had and who were genuine HR gurus. I personally had a measly 2,000 Twitter followers, but some of my influential HR friends were among those 2,000 followers, and *they* had tens of thousands of people following them. This meant that asking a handful of favors could see our content retweeted to hundreds of thousands of people from our audience, with the added bonus of an implicit recommendation from the people who were retweeting.

Hard Work

So we'd become part of the HR tribe and we were focused on the one-two punch of "build the audience, then market to them." What did this actually look like in terms of our day-to-day marketing activities?

We used our developing insider knowledge to create content that was interesting to our audience. Sometimes the content was about Sonar6's product or our philosophy, but often it was about more general topics of interest to HR people. For example, one of the biggest challenges HR faced in the mid-2000s was managing millennials, this whole generation of employees who seemed to function differently in the workplace than the people who'd come before them. So we talked about that, a lot. We made references to pop culture that we were pretty sure our audience would get. We'd try to generate a new piece of content every couple of weeks.

We used this content in two ways. The audience-building part of our efforts focused on very short enticing emails sent to lists (that we had either bought or rented) of HR people who had not yet opted in to receive stuff from us.[14]

---

[14] List purchase or rental is a pretty arcane topic. Generally speaking, you provide a set of the characteristics of the kind of people you want to target (for instance, managers with HR in their title working in midsized businesses) to a list provider (of which there are many), and they'll rent or sell you a list of names and email addresses that match your criteria for an agreed price.

The deal was, they had to opt in to our ongoing mailing list in order to see the full version of the interesting thing we just teased them with. When we got the content and the teasers right, a bunch of the recipients of our unsolicited emails would opt in, absorb the content we sent them and become new additions to our growing audience.

The second way we used our content was to keep this audience of opted-in HR people engaged. Every couple of weeks we sent this list of opted-in people something interesting: a video, a newsletter, an infographic. We tried to mix it up and keep it — yes, you guessed it — a mixture of human, clear, personable and sometimes mysterious.

If this all sounds like hard work, that's because it was. I sometimes asked why we were spending so much time and energy developing content that wasn't about our product, and I'd be quickly reminded that the point was building and maintaining our audience, not selling the product. In Ian's words: This content was the newspaper, not the ads.

But the whole point of building an audience was ultimately to sell our product to them. Much as we came to love the HR tribe, we weren't in the game just to provide them with interesting content. So occasionally we did gently remind them that we actually made software they might like to find out about. We were, however, very careful with our hard-won audience.

As I mentioned earlier, we were obsessive about measuring everything. Our data told us that hard-sell content resulted in a bunch of unsubscribes. After watching this happen a few times, we decided that selling, whether it was an invitation to a product webinar or the offer of a free product trial, would never be more than 25 percent of the dialogue with our audience.

What this meant in practice was that we put a small ad for our product in the corner of a newsletter. Or our audience would get three emails that were just engaging content, and only then would we send them an invitation for a free trial. We hoped our audience would be so enamored of our content that even the end-of-year hard-sell special with our CEO having goop hurled at him wouldn't make their fingers itch to click on "unsubscribe."

Eventually Sonar6 built an audience of tens of thousands of HR people who had opted in to receive our emails because they valued our opinion. Marketing to a primed audience like this is very efficient. In fact, as I came to realize, marketing to an audience of "your people" is efficient enough to make up for the fact that audience building takes all that time and effort upfront. That's it, folks. The one-two punch.

The best thing about this approach is that once you've got an accurate read on your audience, getting the content right isn't that hard. When I was creating content for Sonar6, I'd often think back to that club in Atlanta. I thought about the conversations after the un-conference, after a few drinks, when everyone let their hair down, and I did a mental test: Could this content be a conversation at that venue? If I talked like this would I be inside or outside the circle?

Startup Marketing Hacks #15-17
15. The One-Two Punch.
Having an audience is critical. Most startups can't afford to market to everyone, so marketing becomes a two-step process: 1) build an audience and 2) market to that audience.

16. Audience building is an activity in itself.
An audience is a group of people you have a way of

reaching and who are reasonably likely to be interested in what you have to say. A nice, tight definition of an audience is *the contacts in your database who have opted in to receive communications from your company.*

Audiences are built through content. Content that attracts and retains an audience is often very different from content that actually sells your product. You have to be cool with not always trying to sell.

17. Be Jane Goodall.
Great content speaks to your audience. To do this well you need to be one of the tribe. Spend all the time you can with members of your target market. Join their communities. Go to their parties. Absorb their version of what the world looks like. Count them among your friends.

Sanity check your content by asking the question "If I talked like this to my friends from our market, would I sound like a dick?"

6.
Brave New World

Less of the Why, More of the Who

O, wonder! How many goodly creatures are there here! How beauteous mankind is! O brave new world, that has such people in it!
— William Shakespeare, "The Tempest"

Imagine this is not a marketing book but a pick-a-path adventure story. A very short one.

Get in character: You're in charge of marketing for a startup cookie manufacturer. You're busy planning the launch of a new triple-chocolate cookie. In a dream you're visited by the Deity of Marketing, who bestows upon you this piece of rock-solid consumer insight: "People who drive yellow cars are 10 times more likely to buy triple-chocolate cookies than are people who drive any other color car."[15]

Do you:

---

[15] If there indeed was a god of marketing, I suspect that she would be omniscient, but not omnipotent. Which is the point of this chapter.

a) wake with a start, well before your alarm, and spend a fretful morning trying to understand the nature of the link between yellow-car ownership and consumer preference for triple-chocolate cookies;

or

b) sleep until 10 a.m., eat a leisurely breakfast, then drive to your local supermarket and start putting fliers for your new cookies on every yellow car in the parking lot.

OK, hold that thought. We'll come back to what happens to you shortly. But in the meantime, here's a truncated history of modern marketing.

Thirty years ago marketing was focused on understanding the "why" of consumer behavior. Marketers loved to think about potential customers and put them into target segments: Working Mothers, Young Professionals, Ladies Who Lunch — you know the sort of thing.

Then they would try to work out the behavior of these groups. Marketers borrowed from literature on human psychology and generated all sorts of underlying reasons for why a particular group would or wouldn't respond to a particular approach, would or wouldn't buy a product. And, you know, things sold. Marketing happened. So at least part of it worked.

There was an underlying assumption in the model that different people behaved differently — that not everyone would think about and select products in a category in the same way. Which is good. But it was limited by the technology of the time, which forced marketers to select only a handful of different target groups and then act as if the people within each of those groups all behaved identically. Which, of course, they didn't.

In the past decade or so the mass collection of data and the ability to mine that data for information about individual behavior became a thing. This changed marketing. Dramatically. Hypothesizing about the how membership of a target group would affect consumer behavior was replaced by actionable insights drawn from data. Any insight that reliably predicts behavior — whether for an individual or a dozen prospects or everyone with a yellow car — can be acted on. But most importantly, it can be acted on without really being understood.

Think about that for a second. If I know what will happen, I don't need to care about *why* it happens; I just need to care about *who* makes it happen. That's marketing now. And marketers in startups don't have time to theorize and pontificate. They need to act.

This is a scary change if you're a marketer used to a traditional approach of describing target groups and designing marketing for each of them. Don't get me wrong — there's still plenty of room for target personas and the like in good marketing practice, but think about the power of this brave new world. When Amazon tells me that people who bought "The Tempest" also bought "Faust," this isn't based on a marketer having put me in a target group of "lovers of Elizabethan literature" and then designed a marketing approach. It's purely a data-driven insight.

So back to our adventure. Hopefully the best choice is becoming obvious: Get to the cars! But if you still need convincing, here's the thought experiment that convinced me.

What Does 50,000 People Look Like?

Rowan Simpson was one of our investors at Sonar6. He's an entrepreneur himself who had a phenomenal exit. You know that thing where you assume that someone who has been hugely successful will be arrogant, ruthless and hard-nosed, and then it turns out that they're the just the opposite? Rowan is that guy: softly spoken, generous with his wisdom and with a natural way of putting the complexities of business into everyday language.

Rowan talked to the team one day, and ran through an exercise in visualizing the numbers involved in the business. He talked about when Trade Me, the business he'd been involved in, reached the 50,000-customer mark. At that point, he said, staff would just look at the number and forget what it really meant. "Sometimes," he said, "you need to take a step back and think about what 50,000 people actually looks like. It's a stadium full of people." Try the same thought experiment with your business. Whatever the number of prospects or customers you have, try to picture them all in one place.

That idea had a big effect on how we thought about our business. As soon as you visualize all those people crammed into a stadium, you think about the sheer volume but also the almost endless variation — 50,000 different people, each with their own wants and likes. Their own lives! I remember discussing that presentation with my small marketing team afterward and feeling overwhelmed. *We* had about that many prospects in our database.

Faced with the sheer level of diversity, our efforts at target marketing, based on putting people into tidy groups to predict behavior, seemed pointless. We needed a better approach.

Teach a Man to Phish

"Permit me to inform you of my desire of going into business relationship with you. I got your contact from the International web site directory. I prayed over it and selected your name among other names due to it's esteeming nature and the recommendations given to

me as a reputable and trustworthy person I can do business with and by the recommendations I must not hesitate to confide in you for this simple and sincere business."

Detecting scams on the internet used to be so easy. The polite broken English, the promise of millions, the upfront requests for your bank account details. It was pretty easy to avoid being scammed. So the scammers became more sophisticated. Survey scams, bogus warnings, like-farming scams, lottery scams, overpayment scams, internet dating scams — scammers now use hundreds of increasingly sophisticated tricks to get sensitive information from victims. Fortunately, we're all too smart to share our personal stuff with a faceless internet presence, right?

Except on Facebook. Facebook collects tens of thousands of pieces of information about its users, and it's not just things that we explicitly click "like" on. Anything you post on Facebook is analyzed by algorithms designed to understand as much about you as possible. Even your "private" messages are trawled. You'd be appalled if an email appeared in your inbox asking you for your relationship status, sexuality and religious beliefs, but I'm pretty sure you'll find that Facebook already has those assumptions about you in its database.

How does Facebook have access to this treasure trove of information about you? Because it's set up in such a way that you willingly give it. When you share information on Facebook, you're sharing it with your friends, but you're also sharing it with Facebook, the most successful phishing scheme ever invented. Facebook sells this information to advertisers, who deliver ads to your news feed based on what Facebook has told them about you. In its marketing to advertisers, Facebook provides the example of a hair product manufacturer that can see who complains about frizzy hair in certain weather conditions. That really is gold.

Some people are uncomfortable about this deal, and complain about it (mostly on Facebook). But few end up resisting what's being offered in exchange: all the joy of Facebook, the social validation, the intrigue of seeing your old school friends' carefully curated lives, the opportunity to do light stalking of ex-partners. And it's free, the only cost being sharing all of your personal stuff to be sold to advertisers.

Clearly, as a marketer, I think Facebook's business model is fucking awesome. As a father and a regular schmuck, I'm suspicious that Facebook's business model may run contrary to people's interests. A cynic might observe that Mark Zuckerberg's oft-repeated quote that "privacy is no longer a social norm" is mighty convenient for a business built on people sharing their data. But as a marketer it's GENIUS.

At Sonar6 we learned to do something similar, although on a much smaller scale. One of our early strategies was to give potential customers a free one-month trial of our software. We hoped that letting customers try the product would reduce the sales effort required to close deals. This didn't really work out: It still took a lot of salesperson effort to get customers over the purchase line. But there was an unexpected bonus.

To start the trial, prospects had to enter data to help us configure the software for them. People signing up for our free trials happily told us which industry they were in, how many staff they had and what time of the year they did their annual employee performance reviews — details that were genuinely used by the system to create a trial that matched their requirements. However, we also put these details in our database, and then we used them to market our product more effectively to that prospect. For example, simply knowing what time of year a business did its annual performance reviews helped us target when to put in the most sales effort. If it's May and they do their reviews in November, we know that we can (and should) avoid the hard sell for several months.

Over time we gathered information about the industries and size of organization our audience worked in. We combined this data with their responses to our marketing content to create a picture of what content worked for which prospect. Understanding the role of the prospect in the organization was important too: CEOs respond to very different messages than HR managers do.

This initial approach to collecting and using data grew into a sophisticated strategy designed to get all the information we needed from a prospect to help us to market to them effectively. As time went on we realized that we didn't need to get all the data at once; we could build the relationship and gather more data as we went. The first interaction would be us asking for a name and an email address so we could send the prospect our awesome content. Once we were in email dialogue we started to occasionally seed things like small surveys: By completing a short questionnaire about your HR, you got access to research gathered from many businesses. We eventually worked up to offering a free trial of the software, and by the end of that stage we had a pretty detailed picture of the prospect in our database.

The first step in a data-centric approach to marketing needs to be collecting really useful data on prospects. Build a relationship with customers and prospects where they feel compelled to share information about themselves with you. I'm not ashamed to say it: Marketing is phishing.

Down the Rabbit Hole

So you've collected data on your prospects. What now? Three things: A/B testing, mass personalization and insight gathering. We're going down the rabbit hole for a few pages. Stick close.

A/B Testing

Back at the start of the book, on that fateful Tuesday, we had been A/B testing email subject lines. I'll probably A/B test different titles for this book. It's simply a statistical hypothesis test. Two variants of a piece of marketing, A and B, are tested on a sample from your audience to see which performs better (gets more emails opened, more likes, more shares, more clicks — whatever the measure is). Often this testing is iterative. If variant A wins the first test, then it's refined into two more variations that are tested against each other, and so on.

A/B testing encourages a data-centric approach to decision making that often stretches across the whole marketing discipline and even further into the business. A/B testing values real results from your audience over your assumptions about what you think will work, which is a good thing. At Sonar6 we did *a lot* of A/B testing. Our tagline, "At last, performance reviews that don't suck," went through a dozen iterations before we saw the response rates we wanted.

When we started we didn't have our own large database of prospects to test potential taglines on, but we did have Google AdWords, and this gave us access to a huge number of test subjects. AdWords are the sponsored ads you see at the top of your Google search results. Advertisers bid to have their short ad appear at the top of the search results for specific terms, in our case "performance management software." The advertiser pays Google a small amount anytime someone clicks on the ad.

By spending a modest budget on AdWords, we were able to serve up different versions of potential Sonar6 ads to tens of thousands of HR people (safely assuming that most people searching for "performance management software" were from HR). Then, by measuring which ad got the most clicks, we could make decisions about marketing content based on actual data about what worked with our audience.

We started by trying something like five possible taglines in different genres: Hard-hitting. Awards-focused. Funny. Scientific-sounding. Price-oriented. This was really "A/B/C/D/E testing" since we had five options, but it was the same basic idea — a statistical test of which option worked best for our audience. In the end "Performance reviews that don't suck" was the clear winner, soundly beating out No. 2, which was "Award-winning performance review software."

Now that the votes were in on the first round, we started to iterate. "Performance reviews that don't suck" was pitted against lots of similar variants, with "At last, performance reviews that don't suck" eventually prevailing. And we didn't stop there. We even got down to trying that same tagline with and without an exclamation point (those exclamation points again!). Eventually we settled on "At last, performance reviews that don't suck" (no exclamation point), and it remained with us.

Mass Personalization

So A/B testing, a.k.a. running marketing experiments, is done. That brings us to mass personalization, a deep discipline in itself, much of which is unnecessarily arcane for most startups. But the core premise is very powerful:

Customers' behavior determines the marketing they receive.

The example I've already used is Amazon. At the probably-too-hard-for-startups end of the spectrum is the My Amazon home page, which has tailored offers that are based on my past purchases, my interests, my demographic profile and my location. Amazon selects those offers using complex algorithms and AI that analyzes my past behavior and compares it with other customers' past behavior to try to predict my future behavior.

Like I said, probably too hard for startups. But it's the simplest part of Amazon's strategy that is the most powerful. Remember the bit where Amazon tells me that people who bought "The Tempest" also bought "Faust"? Since I'm looking at "The Tempest," perhaps I'm also interested in "Faust" and a bunch of other old literature?

Thing is, if I need a present for my brother's birthday and start looking at Malcolm Gladwell's "Blink," the recommendations will change, showing me other Malcolm Gladwell books, and related business, economics or pop-psychology-type books, that other people who bought "Blink" have also bought. Helpful. Perhaps Philip will like one of these.

Essentially Amazon lets customers put themselves in groups based on their actions (which products they look at). Customers change groups as often as they change behavior. Offers are delivered to me based on data about the actual behavior of real people who have previously interacted with the Amazon system, not demographics or some other way of classifying potential customers into target segments.

We did plenty of this behavior-based marketing at Sonar6, and it was often very simple. I talked in Chapter 5 about how we would send our audience an email every week or so with engaging, cheerful content about HR topics. We also tracked how often people visited certain pages on our website. We built a switch into the system. If someone started visiting our pricing page frequently, if they started a free trial or if they registered for a product webinar, we flicked that switch and swapped them into a different bucket. They had moved from being part of the general audience to being a sales lead.

Once that switch flicked, we stopped sending light-hearted generalist content every week or so and started sending much harder-hitting emails — about our product, case studies, information on implementation, internal selling tools and competitor comparisons — a couple of times a week. Their behavior changed the marketing they received. That's personalization.

Insight Gathering

This is simply analyzing the data you've collected on customers to see whether there are any patterns that can be used to give you a marketing advantage.

The techniques of insight gathering can get pretty nerdy pretty quickly. This is the zone where AI meets marketing, specifically the application of neural networks. A neural network is basically software that gathers and extracts information from large data sources, identifying cause and effect within the data. They're renowned for telling you what you didn't know that you didn't know. Remember when the Deity of Marketing visited you in a dream about cookies and gave you the insight that people with yellow cars bought more cookies? On closer investigation I'm sure you'd find that the Deity of Marketing got that insight by deploying a neural net.

However, let's focus on the simple startup end of the spectrum. Insight gathering can be as straightforward as sifting through your customer and prospect data to see whether you can find any useful patterns. I mentioned that at Sonar6 we would change our marketing when people either started a free trial, visited our pricing page or attended a webinar. How did we choose these as the flags? By analyzing the data that showed that people who became customers had almost always done at least one of those three things shortly before purchase. It was a predictive piece of insight and we acted on it.

OK, we're back out of the rabbit hole. This is just a taster. A/B testing, mass personalization and insight gathering are deep disciplines of their own. It might be worth going off and researching them more, to understand the sort of technology you will require.

Just don't become a nerd.

The Ghost in the Data

Just because nobody complains doesn't mean all parachutes are perfect.
— Benny Hill

When I was a kid my older brother showed me some research done by a life insurance company. It showed that people who floss their teeth live, on average, about two years longer than those who don't. That's pretty significant. I started flossing my teeth and wondering exactly how this would make me live longer. I eventually concluded that flossing your teeth removed a kind of low-level load on your immune system, and without that load you lived longer.

Actually, as I realized when I learned a little more about statistics, regularly flossing your teeth probably has *no* direct impact on how long you live. However, if you're the sort of person who flosses then you're probably also the sort of person who looks after your health in other ways. You probably exercise, get regular checkups and care about what you eat. So people who floss do, on average, live longer than people who don't, but if any one of those people stopped flossing tomorrow, that wouldn't affect their life expectancy at all. I stopped flossing.

This is an example of the difference between correlation and causation. And we marketers are — let me put this nicely — generally terrible at recognizing this difference. Just because two factors move in lockstep *does not mean* that one causes the other; it just means they're correlated. One may drive the other, or some other factor may drive both of them. Or it may be coincidence.

One of the biggest dangers of a data-centric approach is placing too much emphasis on correlations that come out of the data, when causation is unclear. This problem — reading stuff into the data that isn't really there — existed when marketing data was mainly gathered through expensive and time-consuming telephone or in-person surveys. But it has gotten a lot worse in the age of big data. Suddenly the analysis of large amounts of data (like the information we had gathered on the 50,000 prospects in the Sonar6 database) allows us to generate ever-greater numbers of insights, with the risk of an ever-greater incidence of false confidence. The thing is, lots of data will tend to throw up lots of relationships — many of which are the product of chance, or that are explained by some unmeasured third factor, or that may be genuinely related to each other but not in the way we assume. To quote the brilliant Nat Torkington, "needles are the same size, but the haystack is growing exponentially." Which is to say that the long, thin pointy thing you're holding in your hand might be just a bit of dried grass rather than the metal sewing instrument you think it is.

I explained how at Sonar6 we learned that people who

did a free trial were more likely to go on to become a customer. So there was a correlation between doing a free trial and becoming a customer. Knowing this was useful. It was one of the fundamental pieces of customer insight we used to drive our marketing flow. However, this is a correlation, and only that. There's no causation implied. People who did a free trial were more likely to purchase than those who didn't; however, doing a free trial *did not cause* someone to purchase.

We made this mistake. Armed with the insight that free-trialists were more likely to purchase, we spent *a lot* of resources trying to get more people to do a free trial. We spent money and effort encouraging free trials among people who wouldn't have otherwise started a free trial. And guess what? It didn't increase sales at all.

Marketers, we need to be careful. At Sonar6 we desperately wanted free trials to cause purchases. As product designers and engineers we liked the idea that the experience of trying our product was so good that it caused someone to purchase. But the evidence played out more like this: People decided to purchase for their own reasons, and doing a free trial was just one of the logical pieces of diligence they did as part of that decision.

This example of wanting correlation to imply causation is just one example of what psychologists call *confirmation bias*. It's the tendency that pretty much all humans have to search for or interpret information in a way that confirms what we already believe. Think about that for a second. *We all do it.* The danger in a data-led marketing practice is obvious.

All data-centric marketing needs to be coupled with a very strong dose of critical thinking. Most of us marketers are not statisticians. Be careful when you pretend to be. Always ask this question: *Does the data really show me this, or does this result just make me feel better about what I already think?*[16]

'Angry Birds' and Wild-Eyed Ideas

I was standing in the customs line in LAX Terminal 2. The line meandered left and right, left and right through a long series of those corridors created with retractable belts. It's like lining up at Disneyland, but with none of the joy. Every now and then a muttering uniformed staff member would unhitch a belt from one pole and attach it to another, in some baffling way that created ever-more-complex labyrinths. At any time, people in the line behind you could suddenly be redirected so that they were now in front of you. I was worried that my whole section of the queue was in an endless loop. LAX is its own very special form of stress.

To pass the time I started playing "Angry Birds" on my phone. Remember "Angry Birds"? It has probably had 2 billion downloads. But remember when it was really popular, and when it was still cute rather than annoying?

I noticed the guy in front of me was also playing "Angry Birds." We shared some kind of joke about pesky green pigs. Then the (muttering) woman in uniform came along and told us to stop. Just like a grumpy parent past a kid's bedtime. She pointed at the "No Phones" sign. "But I'm playing 'Angry Birds,' " I mock-protested. Joking with the

---

[16] Inspired by Susan Etlinger's TED talk on big data. "As my high-school algebra teacher used to say, show your math, because if I don't know what steps you took, I don't know what steps you didn't take, and if I don't know what questions you asked, I don't know what questions you didn't ask. And it means asking ourselves, really, the hardest question of all: Did the data really show us this, or does the result make us feel more successful and more comfortable?"

joyless official in immigration ... risky. But her face lit up: "Oh, 'Angry Birds,' don't get me started. I hate that game. I lurve that game." With a few deft movements of retractable belts the line in front of me was cleared all the way to a waiting customs officer. It was like Moses parting the Red Sea.

Every few weeks at Sonar6 the marketing team would get together and throw content ideas around. There was no limit to the wackiness of these conversations. After that LAX experience I had this idea of doing some kind of "Angry Birds" content piece. I was so struck by the game's universal appeal. Only thing was, we made HR software, so the logic of this seemed a stretch. At our content get-together, someone in the team built on this and suggested "Management Lessons from 'Angry Birds.' " It seemed like an absurd idea, but we all agreed to give it a try. Shelly and Karen quickly worked up a quirky web page with about 300 words on how managing a team was a bit like choosing the birds to catapult around on "Angry Birds." It had delightful graphics and all the normal social plug-ins to encourage sharing and opting-in to our other content.

Shelly and Karen did a great job and the work made me chuckle, but it didn't especially stand out from the great work they always did. We started to share it via Twitter, as we often did with new marketing content to get some initial feedback before we passed it to A/B testing. The initial response wasn't huge, but our link to the page was getting retweets. Then it started to build shares on Facebook. For a week the momentum built and we were happy, so we just kind of left it. We didn't bother with A/B testing since it was going so well. Then, all of a sudden, it stopped going well and started to go amazing. The "Angry Birds" content took on a life of its own.

The page ended up with 400,000 views. I know it's easy

to find viral hits with millions of views, but we made HR software, and 400,000 people had viewed our funny little "Management Lessons from 'Angry Birds' " page. We were stoked. The Facebook social plug-in was full of comments like "This nails it," "So true" and "This made me laugh." We were spreading a tiny bit of joy around, which felt lovely, and we were getting opt-ins, lots of them: people signing up, giving us their emails because they wanted more content from us. "Angry Birds" was a hit. But most importantly it was creating sales — plenty of new customers who had first become aware of us because of "Angry Birds."

Why am I telling you this story after all the talk of the importance of data? Because the last thing I want to tell you about data is the most important: Sometimes you need to completely not think about it. Looking at the data — puzzling over A/B testing and exactly when to change your marketing tactics for a given prospect — WILL NOT GIVE YOU ANY IDEAS (or, at least, not on its own).

Taking a data-centric approach is essential in marketing, but it's essentially about refining what you already have. Decent A/B testing and prospect data analysis almost guarantee your marketing will continuously improve. Could I ever develop enough customer insight to realize that "At last, performance reviews that don't suck," drives more action than "At last, performance reviews that don't suck!"? Probably not, and that's exactly why A/B testing is so useful. Over time, and over a big market, those incremental improvements add up to many more customers. But to do great marketing (or even halfway decent marketing) you still need some raw material — some *good* raw material — to work with.

So where does the raw material come from, and how do you identify it at that early stage when you're sitting there with your team and there are 26 wild-eyed ideas for content on the board? The answer is marketing intuition. If you're in marketing and you're at all successful, you must have some spark or basic sense that tells you a certain piece of content or strategy has a chance of working. Then you feed your marketing intuition with three things: the hard data you collect about your prospects, your customers and what works with your existing marketing material; the soft data you collect through becoming part of your customers' tribe; and everything else. Yup, *everything else*. Playing a game standing in line in customs. Going to an art gallery. Playing paintball with the kids. It's the everything else that seeds original, quirky, eye-catching ideas that have people sharing, liking and relating to your content.

Startups have to move fast. You have to make experimental leaps. These leaps will sometimes be successful and sometimes not. Over time, though, your hit rate will get better if you're feeding your intuition right. In terms of marketing content, some of our early hits were just plain mistakes. Remember that bung email I sent back in Chapter 1? The one that started "Dear {FirstName LastName}" and outperformed all our other previous emails? That, obviously, was just a fuckup. But the response told us something, and helped us further develop our intuition. "Throwing things at John" wasn't A/B tested, but we were pretty sure it would work, because we knew — from the hard and soft data we'd internalized — that our HR tribe would love the get-the-boss dynamic and basic physical comedy. Plus, the prospect data told us that our audience would bite on the discount. Later still, when we sat in the room talking about "Angry Birds," we didn't know we'd have a hit on our hands but we did have a strong feeling it was worth a try, and we were right 400,000 times over.

So, in a way, marketing has bifurcated. There's coming up with wild-eyed ideas and sorting through them to work out what to work on. That bit relies on you and your team having decent intuition about your audience, and a decent supply of fresh inputs to generate new ideas. Then there's the data-centric bit, where you incrementally improve your content and hone your strategies, using the data and just the data, not your own hunches, prejudices or whims.

The key is to do both of these things well and to consciously treat them as separate activities. Know when you're doing data-centric marketing and when you're doing wild-eyed ideas. Make each of these its own discipline. Set aside time for both.

Startup Marketing Hacks #18-21

18. Take a kid phishing.

Unashamedly make the collection of individual data part of your marketing process. The more you know about people, the more successful you will be at influencing their behavior.

Get insights from the data to help you develop more effective marketing. See if you can use individual data to predict behavior and work out how to act on it. Use A/B testing to continuously improve. Experiment with simple mass personalization.

19. Always floss your teeth. Or not.

Be careful of confirmation bias. Always ask this question: "Does the data really show me this, or does this result just make me feel better about what I already think?"

20. But don't become a data nerd. They're boring.

Sometimes, when trying to make big leaps in marketing, it's

best to stop thinking about the data. Let your team come up with wacky ideas that come from everywhere but the data. If you've all been paying attention you'll have a sense for what will work.

21. Startup marketing is either data-centric or wild-eyed ideas.

Great startup marketers are good at both using data to continuously improve the performance of their marketing and at using their marketing intuition to create great raw material. Set aside time for both..

7.
White-Coat Marketing

The Meandering Path of Hand-Waving Uncertainty

I first met Bret Starr on the floor of a trade show in Chicago. People kept telling me to seek him out. "How will I find him?" I asked. "Oh, you'll find him" was the universal response. And there he was, walking slowly across the show floor, wearing a bowling shirt with "Bret" embroidered on the pocket. Alongside and behind him trailed a small posse of underlings with matching personalized bowling shirts.

I called out to him. He turned. "Ah, the New Zealanders." Apparently he'd been told to seek us out too. Bret is a gentle giant, with a soft Texas drawl and an infectious laugh. I think of him as a cross between an excited college student and a Southern gentleman. A few years later Bret would come to New Zealand, and despite having not brought his driver's license, he attempted to rent a motorcycle to "get out of the city" for a weekend. I guess you could say he has a lust for life.

"Do you have a piece of paper?" I could barely hear him over the noise on the trade show floor. "I want to draw you something."

There's nothing better than being told exactly what you need to know exactly when you need to know it. Bret was about to draw me a diagram of the active path. You've probably heard of it. I had probably heard of it. But up until that meeting with Bret I wasn't putting it into practice at Sonar6. A three-minute meeting between Bret, John and me on a trade show floor, and a diagram drawn on piece of scrap paper, changed my view of marketing forever.

Up to this point we had done lots of things right in marketing at Sonar6. We had started to build content that broke through the filter. We had a well-developed marketing personality and we had a very clear message with just a hint of mystery. We were building ourselves an audience, and every day we became more native to the HR tribe. We were even becoming more data centric in our decision making.

But.

Our marketing was a hot mess.

And.

Our marketing was a lone dog.

Hot Mess

There's a cliché that gets attached to all sorts of disciplines that goes like this: "Activity X is both an art and a science." Medicine is both an art and a science. Leadership is both an art and a science. Ikebana is both an art and a science.

These examples are all arts because they require creativity and empathy, along with the application of specialist techniques and methods. They're also all sciences because they work best when following a systematic and organized approach that includes evidence-based analysis.

By this definition, marketing is an art and a science. Before that conversation with Bret, marketing at Sonar6 was largely an art — an expensive, kind of hand-wavy art. We had tons of creativity and we were doing great things with brand and audience. But while we were starting to use data to help us make decisions, we lacked any organizing principles, or any ways of clearly understanding what different activities were actually *for* and whether they were successful.

Science requires that you build on your body of knowledge with systematic study. This happens by having a model that's continuously refined by thinking up hypotheses and then proving them or disproving them through experimentation. A/B testing was the closest we got, but otherwise we weren't at all scientific about what we were doing.

The bulk of our marketing strategy went like this: First we'd use AdWords to encourage a free trial. We had some very slick messaging and we were very good at this. Lots of people signed up for our free trials. Then marketing would send a series of emails that tried to convert the trialist into a paying customer. We weren't very good at this. Pre-Bret, we didn't measure how many of these trialists we managed to convert, so I can't tell you exactly how un-good we were at this. But I can tell you that the shout of triumph that signaled a new customer didn't ring out across the team very often.

When we weren't doing AdWords or emailing trialists, we were doing whatever else popped into our heads that we felt might help build our audience. Trade shows, banner advertising, magazine ads, a menu insert at John's cousin Ziggy's burger restaurant (OK, we didn't actually do that, but we probably would have if John's cousin Ziggy owned a burger restaurant). Our marketing looked good and we were frantically busy, but who knew what the hell we were achieving, in terms of customers (cash!) through the door?

Lone Dog
Worst of all (and a sign I should have paid more attention to), the sales team thought marketing had nothing to do with them.

They were mostly focused on calling their way through their own Rolodexes, building their own pipeline and closing their own deals. Marketing was arty waffle, and, for all they knew, actually just a waste of space (and cash!). They didn't see any specific output from what we were doing.

Then Bret happened. It sounds crazy, but talking to Bret was probably the first time we'd started thinking seriously about marketing and sales as part of the same process. Bret's diagram showed a seamless path from a person becoming aware of Sonar6 to becoming a Sonar6 customer. Bam! It was a genuine "aha!" moment, after which we looked at each other and thought "How did we not get that before?"

The Active Path
So here's what Bret scribbled on that piece of paper:

Suspects → *Prospects* → *Leads* → *Customers*

And here's what he said to us: "Suspects are all the people out there who have never heard of you. Prospects are people you're in dialogue with. Leads are people who are going to buy a product like yours soon. Customers, well, they're customers. The job of marketing (and sales) is to move people from one box to the next, left to right, as efficiently as possible. And, by the way, you can really only do that one step at a time. The mistake that everyone makes is assuming you can move people all the way from the left to the right in one fell swoop. Nope. Just move them one step further down the active path toward becoming a customer. That's your job."

One step at a time.

Wow.

That's my job.

Of course.

We went home and rethought our whole approach to marketing. The team wasn't just building audience or raising awareness or managing the brand; *we were moving customers along the path.* Not everyone in your market behaves the same (in fact, no two people do anything exactly the same), but in aggregate, all people in our market followed the stages in Bret's active-path model, though at vastly differing speeds.

So, duh, that's kind of obvious isn't it? Well, yes. But up until that point, no. The goal of sales and marketing at Sonar6 was, of course, to take people who'd never heard of us and eventually sell them our product. That was hard work, and even we didn't really know how we went from, say, great tagline and cute article to cash in hand. The active-path model took that really hard problem and broke it down into steps that seemed more solvable. Instead of trying to take someone from zero to 60, now we saw ourselves as accelerating them through the gears. The active path was an organizing principle for the demand-generating side of the business. Bret gave us science.

As soon as we got back from the trade show, we made a list of all the ways we turned suspects into prospects. This included things like list rental and AdWords, which were of course things we'd always done, but now we thought of them as activities specifically designed to turn suspects into prospects. We put it all down on paper in our version of the active-path model: Not just the four boxes Bret had drawn for us, but also everything we knew about how we were moving people along that path. It was, essentially, our best guess about how our marketing actually worked.

Working on that first version of our marketing model, we had to clearly define the stages. What exactly did we mean by "prospect"? We decided that, for us, a prospect was someone who opted in to receive email from us. So if we didn't have their email address and we didn't have permission to email them, they weren't a prospect.

Then we made a list of the things we did that helped turned prospects into leads, which at this stage was mainly email marketing: newsletters, invitations to webinars and the like.

Leads also had to have a specific definition. In this case, they had to have given us a buying signal: starting a free trial, attending a product webinar or filling out our price-request form.

We drew a chart of those definitions and those activities and that became our very first Sonar6 marketing model.

The Marketing Laboratory

That initial model we created became the organizing principle behind all our marketing, but it couldn't tell us which specific activities would or wouldn't work. That was where experiments came in. Instead of just saying "Let's use list rental now instead of AdWords," we did an experiment to test the effectiveness of AdWords versus list rental.

We started by stating an explicit hypothesis. For example, "A $10,000 investment in list rental will generate at least 1,000 prospects (with email address and opt-in) at an effective cost of no more than $10 each, which is the cost per prospect currently achieved with AdWords." Then we went out via both list rental and AdWords, with matching content, to see whether the hypothesis was correct.

The hypotheses weren't just about the cost of prospects. We also tracked how many of the prospects that we got in different ways ended up turning into leads and customers. It's all very well getting 1,000 prospects, but if only two of them end up as customers it may not be worth it (and it also may be worth refining your definition of prospect!).

Many of our marketing ideas came from customer insight, both data-driven and informal. The beauty of the scientific approach was that we had a framework to test these ideas. At first our main form of communication to prospects was text-based email. Talking to a group of prospects one day, we learned that lots of them liked video content. We made some video and ran an experiment. It worked: We got X prospects at Y cost — as good or better than our existing activities. We started including video.

Some days I really felt like I should slip on a white coat and get out the test tubes and beakers when I arrived at work. OK, maybe not quite, but certainly our part of the office became much less about "Hey, guys, what do you think of this?" and much more about "Here's an idea. How can we test whether it works?" You could say we stopped being a marketing studio and started being a marketing laboratory. We found science.

A marketing model underpins continuous improvement. Customer insight and marketing intuition drive marketing experiments. The more experiments you run, the more customer insight you gain and the more marketing intuition you build. Working like this is extremely stimulating. Rather than being stuck with the tried-and-true, your job becomes:

Think of something plausible, then test it. Does it work? Great! It doesn't? Move on! In the marketing laboratory, stretching yourself is a built-in requirement. It's fun and it's productive — you discover faster, because you try more things out more often.

From Lone Dog to Hunting in a Pack

It's amazing in hindsight, but up until we talked to Bret (two or three years into Sonar6), none of us had ever thought about what the measurable outcome of our marketing efforts was. The active-path model made this suddenly, obviously clear. The prize we were playing for wasn't brand recognition or free trials or likes on Facebook — it was qualified leads[17] for sales to turn into customers. OMG! We were all working on the same thing! Suddenly marketing and sales could see the point of each other.

We started to build a culture where marketing felt responsible to sales to provide leads in the quantity they needed to make the monthly sales targets. Likewise sales got on board with marketing. Sales could see qualified leads coming down the line to them, and could even predict, to some extent, the number and the quality of those leads. Then, miraculously, sales started to feel responsible to marketing. As a salesperson given leads, you knew it fell on you to close those leads at an acceptable rate, or else you were letting down the whole chain.

Thinking about qualified leads as the goal helped us sift through all our marketing activities. Some stuff we did gave us an immediate payoff in qualified leads. Other stuff took longer, but we could see the link. If we couldn't see the link

---

[17] A qualified lead typically means a person who has both the budget to buy what you're selling and a known timeframe to buy it in.

between qualified leads and something we were putting effort into, we seriously questioned why we were doing it. It sounds so obvious. And once we started doing it, it was.

Those four boxes Bret scribbled for us remained the basis of our marketing model even as the business grew to include channels and targeted sales teams and all sorts of other marketing complexity. Which is kind of the point. The active path made the complex understandable.

Eventually our marketing model came to include a few extra boxes and arrows for affiliate programs, outsourced lead generation, sales networking, and so on, but it was always simple enough to understand at a glance — organizing all of our marketing activities in a single view of the stages and dependencies.

Fail Fast: Why Plumbers Are Always Late, and Why They Just Don't Care

"My stepfather was a plumber." The sentence surprised me a little. It exposed a lot more about my dining companion than the normal tightly choreographed theater of Silicon Valley lunch chit-chat usually does. But she was a very successful entrepreneur. Maybe therein lay the difference.

I was rather excitedly relaying the pitch for an early-stage company that I had talked to that morning. They made software for tradesmen, and plumbing featured heavily in their story. The short version was this: Arranging a plumber is a pain. Customers set up a time that suits them, but then the plumber is inevitably delayed and the customer ends up wasting a morning sitting frustrated at home waiting for the plumber to show. By using the tradesperson's smartphone they'd be able to keep track of the plumber's actual location, and that, combined with some other back-end scheduling smarts, meant the customer would be able to easily book a plumber with certainty as to when he or she would arrive. Their pitch to plumbers was obvious: *If you have this system then you'll have happier customers, and happier customers equals more business.* Right? Um, wrong, apparently.

"The problem is that I don't think they understand plumbers," she explained. "I used to work on the phone for my stepdad. His instructions were crystal clear: Whatever time a customer asks for, just say yes."

She went on to explain a few things about plumbers that I'd never thought about. Most people only need a plumber infrequently, so there's not a lot of repeat business. This actually means that in the plumber's business model, customer satisfaction is not necessarily as important as you might expect. Think about it: The frequency of needing a plumber for most people is maybe a handful of times a decade (unless you have particularly problematic pipes). So by the time you need a plumber again you've probably forgotten who you called the last time, regardless of how good the experience was. Moreover, word of mouth barely works; it's been so long since *anyone* last called the plumber!

So what's important? Well, when someone calls, the plumber needs to secure their business. And guess what? Apparently almost everyone who calls wants the plumber first thing in the morning — which is impossible to satisfy. But if the response is an honest "well, I'm sorry, the plumber can't be there at 8:30, but he can be there at 11," the customer will just call another plumber. To solve this, according to my lunch date, plumbers instead agree to whatever time the customer asks for, regardless of feasibility. Losing potential customers because the plumber can't make a preferred time is more immediately damaging to the business than the poor customer satisfaction that results from always showing up late.

As a tech guy I could see the opportunity — a startup using technology to solve an obvious customer problem — but my lunch companion was making a very good point. "I don't think plumbers will want it. I could be wrong. I'm sure plumbing has changed a bunch since I worked for my stepdad, but you'd want to test that stuff pretty early, wouldn't you, before you built too much of the product?"

Fail fast. It's a Silicon Valley mantra for a reason, because tech is expensive. Even this straightforward app to solve a fairly simple customer pain point could easily burn through a seven-figure sum to get to launch. You don't want to find out that tradespeople are going to resist it *after* you've sunk a million bucks.

The same scenario happens with marketing all the time. Marketers sink plenty of resources into big campaigns, and the first signs of success or failure come only after the campaign has launched, when the resources are mostly spent. Making marketing mistakes is OK, but you want to make them quickly and cheaply.

This philosophy runs counter to the way many of us marketers work. It's a natural instinct to try to get everything perfect before you let it go out into the marketplace. We want our marketing to be world-class, so we craft and craft and craft. If this is you or your marketing team, this strategy hurts you. You only get real customer insight when you put something in front of potential customers. *You can't steer a ship that's not moving.* Start to get that feedback rolling in. Whether it's something as simple as a new tagline or as complex as a new product feature, test it quickly.

Minimum Viable Marketing

The idea of fast failure was born out of the work of Eric

Ries, author of "The Lean Startup." He was specifically talking about the development of new products, but his concepts also apply to startup marketing.

Much of startup marketing is trial and error: *You try something. If it works you keep it; if it doesn't work you try something else.* In a trial-and-error world, the one who can find errors the fastest wins. You'll see this fail-fast philosophy recut many ways in startup parlance. Ries called it "lean." Kent Beck and other programmers call it "agile." And Jason Jennings and Laurence Haughton famously captured the startup spirit with "It's Not the Big That Eat the Small … It's the Fast That Eat the Slow." Whichever way you phrase it, the idea is clear: Find out which of your assumptions are wrong by getting feedback from customers as soon as possible. And do it all the time.

In the sphere of new products, this is done by launching the minimum viable product. To quote Ries, "the minimum viable product is that version of a new product which allows a team to collect the maximum amount of validated learning about customers with the least effort."

What if you could apply the same idea to your marketing? Imagine *minimum viable marketing*. In a world of minimum viable marketing, all initiatives start with two questions:

What is my riskiest assumption?

What is the smallest experiment I can do to test this assumption?

Groupon is a global e-commerce marketplace, connecting millions of customers and merchants all over the world. It has incredibly deep technology and complex marketing. It's hard to imagine what it must have been like when it was a startup, but in a wonderfully candid interview on Mixergy, Groupon founder Andrew Mason shed some light: "All we did was we took a WordPress blog and we skinned it to say Groupon and then every day we would do a new post." They'd then just use Apple Mail to email out the coupons people bought. He goes on to summarize it in his inimitable way: "It was totally ghetto."[18]

But the point is they were taking their *riskiest assumption* — that customers would grasp the idea of offers at local restaurants, tell their friends about them and buy them — and then did the *smallest experiment* that tested the assumption: a WordPress website and some emails. Mason goes on: "It was so cobbled together. It was enough to prove the concept and show that it was something that people really liked."

It was *minimum viable marketing*.

There are many more wonderful examples from startup folklore of minimum viable products and marketing. Timehop, an app that tells you what you were doing a year ago today by trawling your social media accounts — Instagram, Facebook, Twitter and so on — originally started as an email. You registered and it would send you an email of your Foursquare check-ins from a year ago. There are also plenty examples of brute-force attempts at proving the riskiest assumption. I lost track of the number of B2B SaaS companies I've seen that have started by largely just describing their new service on a series of slides and then getting in front of corporate customers, not for feedback but to actually try selling a future concept.

In fact, many of the most successful Kickstarter campaigns hinge around minimum viable marketing. A short video is created that describes an as-yet-incomplete product, and effectively tests the go-to-market message. If people like the message they put money into the Kickstarter fund, and money is of course the best

---

[18] http://mixergy.com/interviews/andrew-mason-groupon-interview/

validation available that your assumptions are correct. The flipside, however, is also useful. If the Kickstarter campaign is unsuccessful then you have effectively failed fast.

Finally, it's worth emphasizing that minimum viable marketing is different from asking customers what they want. Henry Ford famously said that "If I had asked people what they wanted, they would have said faster horses." The point of minimum viable marketing is not to ask customers what they want; it's to identify and then test your riskiest assumption in the cheapest possible way. In the example about plumbers, there are plenty of risky assumptions in the model. One of the riskiest that would have surfaced early in the minimum-viable-marketing approach would get framed something like this: "A critical mass of plumbers will want to implement this for their customers."

There are lots of ways of testing this assumption, but one of the cheapest ways is probably brute force: Create a list of plumbers, possibly even in a single neighborhood, then get in front of them and pitch the solution. If your assumption is proved wrong, you failed fast. But if they seem interested, run the next the experiment to test your next riskiest assumption.

This Ain't No Fad Diet

The last comment I have about minimum viable marketing is this: It's iterative. It's not a one-off; it's a way of life. There's a difference between being scientific and treating marketing like a science. A/B testing is being scientific. It's using the experimental method and hard data to make better decisions. But treating marketing like a science requires more — a marketing model with ongoing experiments, each of which improves your model. Marketing turns into a series of experiments, where each experiment is designed to generate more customer insight, and builds on the outcomes of the previous experiments.

When we first started Sonar6, we described our product as a talent-management system. We got that out there in front of the world, and almost no one seemed to notice us or understand us, let alone buy our product. We tried to sell it to lots of people through brute-force minimum viable marketing, and we quickly learned that the term "talent management" was just not part of the day-to-day lexicon of most of our target market. Sure, you might read about that term in Harvard Business Review, but HR practitioners, our potential customers, didn't actually use it.

Big problem.

But not really.

Because in trying to sell to our potential customers, we began to understand their language. Something they did talk about all the time was annual performance reviews. Performance reviews weren't quite what we did, but it was close enough. We repositioned our marketing to go after performance reviews before we made any changes to the product. We started experimenting with Google AdWords and new landing pages to see if we'd convert more suspects into prospects with performance-review-related keywords rather than talent-management-related keywords. Turns out we did. So that was that. We repositioned Sonar6 as a performance-review system, and started configuring the product to support the new messaging.

I remember being worried that we'd confuse the market when we made this pivot. One day our system did one thing (talent management); the next the same system apparently did something different (performance reviews). But then someone reminded me that we were only so far successful in engaging a handful of customers. The market I was worried about was largely imaginary. When you're a startup, the potential market is so big in comparison to the small reach of your marketing that even the grandest failed marketing experiment is immediately forgotten. It's like your marketing has a built-in Ctrl-Z. Don't be afraid to use it.

Startup Marketing Hacks #22-25

22. *Treat marketing as an endless series of experiments.*

Get your science on. Marketing is a race, and you need to gain validated customer insight as fast as possible. Treat every marketing activity not just as an exercise in getting customers but also as a test that tells you more about how your potential customers behave.

23. *Build a marketing model.*

Build a model that describes your best guess of the phases that your customers go through, from becoming aware of your product right through to buying it, and of the activities you undertake to move them through those phases.

24. *Work in a marketing laboratory.*

Test everything in the model. Do existing marketing activities do what you want them to? Can you measure their impact? Treat all new marketing activities as experiments: If they work, add them to the model. Your model is always a work in progress.

The best marketing activities fulfill *two* objectives: They sell more stuff and they increase your understanding of your market.

25. Momentum is more important than perfection.

You can't steer a ship that isn't moving. You learn the most about your marketing when it's in front of potential customers. Get stuff out early and refine it later.

Embrace the concept of minimum viable marketing. Start all marketing initiatives with two questions:

What is my riskiest assumption?

What is the smallest experiment I can do to test this assumption?

8.
The Pac-Man Conundrum

Hot Wheels

I could smell smoke coming out of my suitcase. I had told Mark this would happen. I needed to wrap the presentation up quickly and get off the stage.

Six months earlier, John had started his own small campaign of writing comments on the blogs of influential HR players as part of our initial strategy to join the HR tribe. One of those blogs was by a guy named Jim Holincheck. Back then Jim was a senior analyst at Gartner, an important tech industry research company. We were small, new and totally not on Gartner's radar, but John struck up a conversation as only John can. Eventually he convinced Jim to check out what we were cooking up at Sonar6, and Jim liked what he saw. In fact, Jim liked Sonar6 so much that he nominated us as a Gartner Cool Vendor.

That year, 2007, was the first time Gartner ran a Cool Vendors session at its annual symposium in San Francisco. The Gartner Symposium is a big deal: 5,000 attendees from around the world at a huge conference about technology. Cool Vendors was a breakout session showcasing four hot new technologies. Sonar6 was named the coolest vendor in the Finance and Human Capital Management category.

Because it was a breakout session the room only held about 500 people, but people are attracted to what's cool, vendors or otherwise, and the room filled quickly. In fact, by the time I arrived back from my pre-presentation bathroom stop, they had closed the doors. Sorry, no more space. Once I explained my way into the full room, I took a big gulp of the humid air. "Man," I thought to myself, "I hope my suitcase full of cobbled-together servers doesn't overheat."

We wanted to live-demo our most recent Sonar6 release. But for some reason the Gartner Symposium didn't have internet access that was anywhere near fast enough for a slick presentation. Unperturbed, Mark had cobbled together a small stack of portable servers that resembled a miniature version of our Rackspace production servers, coupled it with a power board and a Wi-Fi router, and then jammed the whole lot into a wheeled suitcase with a power cable hanging out of it. All I needed to do was come in early, plug the suitcase in somewhere near the stage, connect to its Wi-Fi signal and demo the latest version of Sonar6 via my laptop. The only problem with cramming all of those electronics into a suitcase is that they collectively generate a lot of heat. It's normal to put that sort of hardware in an air-conditioned server room, not a suitcase. But in a startup you thrive on danger, right?

Right.

Before the main doors opened, I plugged the suitcase in just below the stage and nipped out to take my bathroom stop. When I came back in, the room was so full that people were sitting all around my suitcase, cross-legged on the floor at the front of the stage like kids at a magic show. At least they'd be warm.

The presentation itself was just bizarre. I was second. First was a guy demonstrating wireless charging. He had something that looked like a fruit bowl and he threw his iPod, his camera and his phone in the bowl, where they all magically started charging. This still seems pretty neat nearly a decade later. The room made this collective "ooh" sound, as 500-plus geeks let out a simultaneous gasp. Wow, that was just the first presentation! Imagine what would be coming next!

HR software from New Zealand, that's what!

I'm sure on some level we deserved to be there. Sonar6 took one of the world's least interesting software categories and completely rethought it. But, standing up there, I felt like I was showing off a reworked bicycle when the guy before had arrived in his flying car. Plus I had the added pressure of the hot suitcase, squatting ominously among the innocent nerds.

My presentation was eight minutes long. I practiced to the second. Getting this right was a big deal. At minute four I smelled smoke. Or I thought I did. You know that weird, hot electrical smell? But I was in the zone, and I didn't let it panic me. At minute six the people sitting cross-legged around the suitcase started realizing something was up. I could see them trying to shuffle away. For an instant I thought about this blowing out of control, about someone shouting "*bomb!*" — but people are strange, and instead of saying anything they all just let the smoking suitcase be. I, however, had completely lost my train of thought, and my beautifully rehearsed presentation was gone. I went into this confused sort of ad-lib and then people were clapping, and then I was done.

I walked casually to the front of the stage, bent down as

if to take a bow, unplugged the suitcase, then walked off. I retrieved the suitcase later. I can't remember the next presentation, although it was probably a personal jetpack. What I do remember was opening the suitcase back at my hotel. I couldn't get the zipper open because the entire plastic lining had melted during the presentation, then hardened again as I tugged the suitcase around behind me for the rest of the afternoon. I sat back, looked at the wreckage and thought "I'm not sure that thriving on danger is really me."

After Gartner, though, the phones started ringing. We'd made it up over the horizon and onto the map as a vendor that people looking for an HR software solution should check out.

It was all because John started commenting on Jim's blog.

Searching for Lumpiness

Shortly after we raised our first round of capital at Sonar6, we found some research about where HR people looked for information about HR software. We now had money to spend on marketing, and this seemed like a godsend to help us plan how to spend it. The nub of the research was summarized in a pie chart. A pie chart that looked like Pac-Man.

What's the answer to the question "I need to find information about X; where should I look?" The answer always seems to be the same: Google. Google is the place where everyone gets information about everything, 75 percent of the time. Make that 75 percent a yellow pie chart, turn it on a jaunty angle, and there you have it: Pac-Man.

Sitting there at Sonar6 HQ, having never really tried to

market the product with any sophistication before, the secret to success seemed obvious: Google. Seventy-five percent of our potential customers go to Google to get information on our type of product. So we needed to be in there. We needed to win Google.

How do you do that? There are really only two ways: search engine optimization (SEO) and search engine marketing (SEM). (It's funny that people still say "search engine" instead of just saying "Google," but that's a different point.) SEO is about making sure your website ranks highly in natural search; SEM is paying for sponsored search results, also known as Google AdWords.

SEO can do a lot to optimize your website, but how well you rank in natural search basically comes down to how much of a reputation you have in your field, which makes natural search pretty difficult for an unknown startup. So you're essentially stuck doing Google AdWords.

AdWords is a big part of the genius behind Google's success. Google displays advertising alongside its natural search results. The advertisers pay every time someone clicks on their link. Because some search terms are more valuable than others, rather than set a standard price for keywords Google has an automatic auction system that determines the price of each term.

Imagine you want an ad for your cookie shop to show up when someone searches for "cookies in Auckland." If you were the only company going after that phrase it would be relatively cheap, but if there were dozens of businesses chasing those keywords the price would go up.

Usually all your competition will also be trying to hit Google. Which means that the price of keywords just goes up and up. When we were doing AdWords at Sonar6, the cost per click for our best keywords in our best markets reached about $14, which was the point at which we no longer made any real money. I remember talking to a guy in Germany about the same thing. He made refilled inkjet cartridges, and guess what, his cost per click was 70 cents, which was the point at which *he* no longer made money.

In economic terms this kind of Google auction creates what is known as "perfect competition": There are no barriers to compete and every competitor for clicks has access to all information. The competitive environment is metaphorically flat — it's a wide-open plain. From anywhere one can see everything; there are no hills to hide behind or valleys to lurk in. It's the sort of environment that suits big, powerful predators, but doesn't suit small startups! Startups thrive in places that aren't flat — places with nooks and crannies. The opposite of flat is lumpy. In a lumpy market there are still inefficiencies such that having some inside knowledge or additional insight can give you an advantage. Hence startup marketing is a search for lumpiness.

Here's the thing. When you're a little startup, you're highly unlikely to be the most efficient player in your market. Somewhere out there are competitors that have the scale, experience or whatever to serve customers at a lower cost than you do. Those players are also going after your keywords on Google. But they can pay more for their advertising and still make money, because they're more efficient than you are. In our case there were HR software companies out there that could pay $14 for those clicks and make a profit. But we couldn't. And after a while we just had to face that fact. We couldn't afford AdWords. But! But, but, but, but, but, but! Seventy-five percent of people find out about products like ours through Google. This forced exactly the question that all startups should ask: *What can we do instead of AdWords?*

I remember writing that very question on the whiteboard

in my office. It just seemed like the most unsolvable marketing puzzle ever. The answer was staring me in the face. *Focus on the "not-Pac-Man."* If 75 percent of our market went through Google that meant that 25 percent *didn't*. The market for performance management software at that point was about $2 billion annually. That meant that there was still a $500 million market that didn't use Google. We just needed to zoom in to the other slivers of the pie chart: social media, blogs, HR websites, magazines, professional memberships, trade shows and so on.

Going back to the research about where HR people looked for information, 5 percent of survey respondents said their main source of information was blogs. Five percent of a $2 billion market is still a $100 million market. Plenty big enough for a startup, at least to begin with. So we targeted blogs. We gathered a list of the influential blogs in our marketplace, and John started posting carefully thought-out comments and getting involved in discussions. Which, eventually, led to me being on the stage at the Gartner Symposium with a suitcase full of melting plastic.

We got better and better at targeting blogs — not just commenting, but actively working with bloggers. Eventually we worked our way around most of the other "not-Pac-Man" segments of the chart. We did LinkedIn HR groups, then trade shows, then HR websites, learning as we went.

The important point is that we steered away, as much as we could, from the mainstream where all our big competitors were, and where we had no real weapons to fight back against their size and deep pockets. Blogs were ideal for us, because there were a loose collection of people with no real mechanism for charging us for the value they could provide, rather than one big company that had figured out how to extract maximum value for its service

(Google).

Facebook was still pretty new when we started, and it was focused on building membership rather than monetization. We used it extensively, because no one else in our market was and because it was cheap to get reach, so long as your content was good. We eventually got to 25,000 followers, which is a pretty decent number considering we made HR software. As it has matured Facebook has become a lot slicker about charging for the value it creates. It's harder to make Facebook work for a startup now, but it's worth looking for new platforms that are still in the phase of building users rather than monetization.

When Facebook was new, it effectively cared more about how our content could attract users to it rather than the profit it could make from us by charging us to communicate with its users. In the early days of paid placement on Facebook, some things were a great value and some weren't. Paying for sidebar ads to attract users was of great value in some of our geographic markets and of poor value in others. At that stage Facebook didn't charge page owners to distribute their content onto the walls of users who liked their page, so we could get content out encouraging Facebook fans to visit our site almost for free. There was a certain *lumpiness* to the value we could get out of Facebook. And not all marketers understood the value across the platform. So the value was lumpy, and we could get some great deals. This is typical of earlier-stage social platforms, where the drive for users outweighs the drive for profit. As a marketer you can make that work for you.

There is, of course, a long line of social platforms that have been applied to marketing, probably starting with GeoCities banner advertising, through MySpace, Facebook, Twitter, Instagram and Pinterest; it's a moveable feast. But the point remains: Newer platforms are likely to be lumpier and work better for startups, and it's also worth searching for lumpiness within platforms that are starting to monetize. If you're reading this book anytime much past the day it was published, this next statement will probably sound quaintly out of date, but Snapchat, Medium blogs and LinkedIn Pulse are all being used efficiently by marketers taking advantage of that early lumpiness now. When it comes to broad social platforms, look carefully at the current generation.

This isn't about avoiding AdWords or other established platforms forever. It's about always looking for alternative marketing channels, and particularly about doing this when you're small, and starting out, and inefficient and low on cash. Once we began really scaling the business, we adopted AdWords with enthusiasm. But by then we had made so many elements of our business so efficient that we could afford to pay $14 per click and still make money.

Know Your Limits

In his wonderful book "How Music Works," David Byrne describes how, when he first formed Talking Heads, the band played venues like CBGB in New York. Small, dark bars, filled with drunk people out for a good time. The performers had to play loud enough to be heard above the racket. He found himself subconsciously writing music that specifically suited that sort of venue.

He goes on to suggest that most genres of music take on a set of standard characteristics based on the environment they were created for. Medieval church music has simple harmonic forms because big churches reverberate so much that anything else would sound horrible. Percussive African music is played outdoors, where there's no reverberation to mush together the intricate layered rhythms of the drums. The percussion is substantial enough to carry over the sound of people dancing and milling around in a big open space. Even recorded music has grown to fill the forms available. The three-and-a-half minute pop song that sounds so natural to us now is most likely the result of original 72 rpm records being about 3.5 minutes per side.

Marketing is a creative endeavor within very established patterns. As a marketer, it's important to understand the parameters within which you can be creative. For example, the structure of TV ads is standard, designed to grab attention in a 30-second spot surrounded by other ads. Most successful TV ads run to one of a handful of patterns. Once you know those patterns, they're very recognizable. The repetition/break is my favorite. It is a series of repetitions followed by a surprise that breaks the pattern, like the Mastercard "Priceless" ads. Next time you watch TV, if you're someone who still does that, look out for this pattern.

As a marketer in a B2B enterprise software business like Sonar6, I needed to know how to be creative within several defined structures. Creativity in 140 characters on Twitter: OK, that structure is pretty easy to understand. Creativity on a web page: Gosh, there's a ton of standard things, but constraints are the midwife of good design. Menu at the top. Logo top left that links back to the home page. Full-width graphic at the top. Columns of content below. Features never bigger than the size of a beer coaster. The list goes on. Do any of these things differently and people will be confused or it will just look wrong.

Standard patterns can change over time. When we built our first web page at Sonar6, we were criticized because the links weren't blue and underlined. And that criticism was correct, because, in 2006, if your links weren't blue and underlined then users wouldn't realize they were links, which is the whole point. You want your creativity to be digestible and provoke action, and if your overarching structure doesn't fall into established patterns it's often just too difficult for the consumer to know where to start. In 2018, if your links are blue and underlined you look sort of … retro, I guess. It's certainly not required anymore.

Marketing Is the Expanding Foam of Creative Endeavor

It's vital to understand the limits you work within, but not just so you can obey them. Sometimes the point is to understand the rules and break them on purpose. Marketing is the expanding foam of creative endeavor — as the context around you changes, there are new gaps and niches for marketing to fill. Your job as a marketer is not just to be good at figuring out how to make the best of the existing patterns; it's also to see the opportunities to do things completely differently.

At the start of the 1990s, most TV advertisers were focusing on 30-second ads and figuring out what they could do that was interesting and creative within that structure. The battle was fought in prime time.

Meanwhile, a bunch of personal-development products (like the Thighmaster) took over TV downtime with long-form infomercials. Suddenly there was a completely new set of rules for marketers: hourlong ads that slowly built to direct action, where the audience was compelled to pick up the phone and order right then. A $200 billion industry was spawned. The infomercial phenomenon wasn't born from trying to get a better result from the existing 30-second paradigm. It was something quite different. First there was cheap TV time available; a gap waiting to be filled. Then marketers started thinking about how to fill it. The resulting infomercials perfectly fit the '90s, but also resembled the sponsored hourlong soap operas of a previous era.

One of the things I'm most proud of in our marketing at Sonar6 was our invention of the *color paper*. To understand what a color paper is, let's first talk about white papers. In British government parlance, a white paper is some kind of authoritative report that informs readers concisely about a complex issue and presents the issuing body's philosophy on the matter, to help readers understand the issue and make a decision. But sometime over the past few decades that very British, very government term was appropriated by business, where it came to mean longish published content intended to persuade potential customers to a particular point of view. A white paper's positioning as being researched and authoritative made it perfect for thought-leadership-based marketing. The idea, I'm guessing, was that a multipage, dry and typically colorless paper was just academic enough to momentarily transcend the puffery of normal marketing and instead be considered impartial expert advice.

At Sonar6, we called that idea out as being highfalutin nonsense that suited the attention span of no one. Instead of dull 2,000-word reports, we created *color papers*. These had much shorter content (always less than 400 words) and a page filled with colorful graphics, even cartoons, that got most of the message across visually. The popularity of this content was astounding, and as time progressed the graphics began to dominate. We still had strong, pithy messages with opinions backed by research, but we presented this in a very graphical way. The same sort of idea got taken to the next level elsewhere, and infographics had their time in the sun as the B2B content gold standard.

Marketing: the expanding foam of creative endeavor.

Sure, your time is stretched, but set aside a part of your schedule every month to think about what you're doing that is genuinely new. In 10 years' time, the cutting-edge marketing stuff you are doing now, feeling good about, it will be done by marketing robots. Seriously. You'd better think of something.

Startup Marketing Hacks #26-29

26. When everyone else zigs, zag.
If you only ever do the same things as your competitors then you're a shitty marketer.

27. Solve the Pac-Man Conundrum.
Google AdWords is a very competitive place to try to find customers. Ask yourself: "What can we do to get customers other than through Google?"

Most markets are big enough that there will be enough other ways for a startup to get to customers. For example, you can focus on emerging social sites that are still focused on adding users rather than monetization.

Eventually you might have to rely on AdWords, but realize that once that's the case, everything else in your business will have to be more efficient than your competitors if you are to make real money.

28. Respect established patterns.
Most marketing falls into a series of patterns. You get to be creative only within the pattern. For instance, a website has a series of standard layout features that consumers understand. If your creativity breaks those standard features, many consumers will not be able to work your website.

29. Do something new.

There's still room for completely new ways of going to market. Set aside some of your time every month to think about what you're doing that's genuinely new.

9.
Sales Isn't Magic

An Elegant, Post-Rationalized Lie

"Successful" is a relative term. I'm sure some of my mates who I grew up with, playing in bands and riding bicycles and chasing girls, think I've had limitless (possibly undeserved) glory, while I've also mixed in circles where any exit under a billion dollars is considered second rate.

But here's the rule: If a group of people think you've had business success, a subset of that group will ask you for business advice. Which you should happily give. However, you should also be aware of the contingent nature of advice: The only thing balancing the amount of awful advice I've received is the amount of awful advice I've given. With that in mind, I always start my advice like this: *Most important business decisions are made out of necessity and most advice is just nostalgia.*[19] We all rationalize our decisions based

---

[19] This may be a paraphrase of the Baz Luhrmann song "Everybody's Free (To Wear Sunscreen)."

on their outcomes. If we do something and it's a roaring success, we tend to exaggerate the level of strategy involved in the decision. I'll give you an example.

At Sonar6 we became known for our automated marketing. We created a big marketing engine that provided a lot of leads to a relatively small sales team. This was a good model for business-to-business growth, and I would often get asked about our sales and marketing strategy. Here's what I would say: When Sonar6 was about 2 years old, we analyzed our sales cycle. Sales cycle in a B2B business is the time from when someone (a prospect) becomes aware of your product to when they purchase your product. At Sonar6 our average sales cycle was about seven months, although it varied. This was a problem. When I talked to the salespeople they all had plenty of deals they were working on, but closing them seemed to take far too long. So long, in fact, that it was killing the business. We were a startup! We would run out of cash before even half these deals were closed.

We decided to hire more salespeople, to help us speed up the sales cycle. More salespeople meant more interaction with prospects, resulting in deals closing faster. At least that's what we hoped. The problem was that even once we had grown the sales team from two to seven, the sales cycle stayed the same — it still took about seven months. Only now we had a lot more money being spent on salespeople. It felt like a mistake. We had hired too many salespeople. I kept tripping over them. They were annoying, with their shiny shoes and their loud voices.

Eventually we had a revelation: *We were focusing on the wrong thing.*

Years ago I worked on a consulting gig with a wily old former Marine named Rob Abshire who, post-service, had built himself a successful practice consulting to manufacturers of consumer durables. The first day I met him he told me he had only one rule of marketing: "People will do pretty much what they were going to do, pretty much when they were going to do it. All marketing ever does is work around the edges." I'm not sure if I agree with that entirely, but for the purposes of our sales and marketing strategy at Sonar6 this was bang on.

Think of marketing as a big machine with a bunch of levers. You put all of your efforts into pulling those levers in the hope that they'll shift consumers' behavior. Some of these levers are more effective than others. And I can tell you now that pulling the lever marked "hurry up and buy" is pointless. No matter how hard you pull that lever, prospects will still do pretty much what they were going to do when they were going to do it.

In retrospect it's blindingly obvious. Imagine you're a prospect thinking about buying a piece of HR software. You're marching to your own beat made up of all sorts of things internal to yourself and your business that drive your behavior. For example, if you do your performance reviews in December and it's May, no amount of calls from a salesperson is going to make you buy performance-review software before about October.

We realized that if we were going to get the machine to do what we wanted — get more sales faster — we were going to have to pull different levers. We decided that the best lever to pull was the one marked "get more people in the pipeline." Basically once we accepted that we couldn't really change the internally driven timelines of individual prospects, we realized that to make the business work we had to get more prospects in the pipeline, and assumed that, because some of them would buy faster than others, scale would solve our problem.

Once we had more prospects, we had to build the

lowest-cost-possible way of nurturing them, and so our automated marketing model was born. As our automated marketing became more and more effective, we found that the point at which a prospect became worth approaching with a salesperson was later and later in the sales cycle. Eventually the leads we were passing from automated marketing to sales were so well-developed that the salesperson, instead of dealing with the prospect for seven months on average, would only have to deal with them for a few weeks. So we didn't need so many expensive salespeople. The business was transformed. I stopped tripping over salespeople; now I was tripping over marketers, with their red-framed glasses and their desks decorated with Japanese toys.

Anyway, the purpose of this story is not to tell you about how brilliantly we conceived and executed our transformation from a sales-led to a marketing-led business. The purpose is to tell you that this whole story, which I have told numerous times, is largely a fiction. It's an elegant, post-rationalized lie.

The reality is this: It was 2008 and the start of the global financial crisis. We weren't selling the product as quickly as we had planned and we had to cut costs in order to avoid running out of cash. We did a quick analysis of the operating expenses of the business and, because salespeople were the most expensive resource and we had seven of them, we cut from that team. With almost no salespeople, we were forced to find another way to build business, and hence we had to start automating our marketing. We couldn't afford to do it any other way.

Like I said, most important business decisions are born of necessity, and most advice is just nostalgia.[20]

---

[20] Except the advice to always wear sunscreen. The long-term benefits of

It's the Math, Stupid

I grew up watching 1970s sci-fi TV. There's a common trope (tropes!) in lots of those shows that goes like this: The "Star Trek" cast arrives at a paradisiacal planet. Everything there is great. Just as you start to relax it turns out that something is badly wrong. It's not paradise at all; in fact it's the complete opposite. It's a living hell.

Running a startup is like living that trope over and over. Whenever things seem perfect, when the staff are happy and the product is working, you get this niggling feeling in the back of your mind that it's all a trap. That any minute now everything that you thought was good will turn out to be an illusion.

The big problem when hiring salespeople is that they're good at selling. Even a mediocre salesperson can make something mediocre sound appealing, including themselves. We had our fair share of false starts with salespeople at Sonar6, but Peter Romeyn seemed different. He showed up at the office with his boxer and his mouth full of teeth and he hit the phones hard. By the way, "boxer" isn't some kind of sales euphemism. Peter actually had a boxer dog called Boston that he brought to the office. Every office needs a dog. Peter himself is Dutch. A Dutchman with a German dog named after an American city in New England. Perfect. Almost too perfect.

For the first few weeks Peter was the model sales guy. Punctual. Professional. Polite. Persistent. In fact, he was raising the whole tone of the office. Then, just like in that episode of "Star Trek," things changed. Peter stopped showing up at the office. Man! I knew it. Sure, he'd occasionally come in briefly on a Thursday or a Friday, but

---

sunscreen have been proven by scientists.

seemingly always when I was in a meeting. I never got a chance to quiz him on what was going on. After several weeks of this I finally cornered him in the kitchen. "Peter," I said, "we need to talk."

"Good," he said. "I need to talk to you too. Shall we go to Allpress?" Allpress was our local café. Don't you just hate that salesperson swagger? Here I was, wanting answers, and he'd somehow just defused the whole situation and now we were going for coffee.

At the café Peter took out a spreadsheet he had printed out. There were three columns, each with successively fewer entries. "This column is all of the businesses I have made contact with. This column is the businesses I have demoed to. This column is the ones where I think I can close a deal this month."

He'd done the calculation on how many calls he was making to get a demo, and how many demos he needed to get a closeable deal. Then he worked backward. "Once I get to demo, I know I've got about a one-in-three chance of closing. But, to get someone willing to demo, I need to make about 35 phone calls. So to get to my quota of four deals a month I need to make 100 calls a week. That eats up the first three days of the week. I'm finding it much easier to get through those calls at home."

Oh. Turns out Peter was the real deal after all. A meticulous salesperson who went on to be an absolute star of the business.[21]

That conversation at Allpress Café changed my view of sales. Up to that point I think I thought that sales was some kind of magic, and incomprehensible to those outside the

---

[21] Peter is also the person who taught me this supposedly Dutch expression about distributing bad news: "If you have to eat a shit, don't nibble it."

process. But it's not. It's just an exercise in probability and math, combined with perseverance and resilience. Oh, and a good process. Hey, that sounds a lot like marketing.

Sales Is a Process

It's easy to say that every sale your business makes is different. All customers have different needs, different ways of thinking, different decision-making processes. But I call bullshit. Sure, while some things are different from one sale to the next, the vast majority of things are the same. And if the vast majority of things repeat, they should be turned into a process.

Here's an interesting exercise for your sales team. Ask them this: *You've finally got a new lead on the phone. What's the very best thing to say to them?* Let's think for a second about it. What's the purpose of that first connection? To get one tiny step closer to selling the product. So that opening statement needs to be something that gets the dialogue going. A question! Sure. But not a yes-or-no question; an open question. In fact, any statement that invites an open response is good.

At Sonar6, our opening statement was "Tell me about your performance reviews at {company name}." It was a great statement because it got people talking immediately about what was good or bad about their performance reviews. Sometimes they'd tell us that they didn't do them, and that was OK too. It was all useful intel.

Once we settled on that first statement, we talked about what to say next based on different responses. This exercise wasn't about creating a strict script; it was about realizing that the sales process could go down a few different paths but lots of similar stuff happened along the way, so we might as well be prepared for it.

Every step of the sales process was honed to help move the lead closer to becoming a customer. We eventually ended up with standard ways to handle most steps and most objections. This ranged from a set of answers to common objections through to specific content that we provided at different points along the way. For instance, we knew that most HR people would eventually need to get the buy-in of others in the organization before making a final decision. At the right point in our discussion with them, we sent them our internal sales guide: a document with specific arguments to convince CEOs, CFOs and others why Sonar6 would be good for the business. We even went as far as creating a handy, and largely unbiased, guide to our competitors, for when the leads we were speaking to needed to do due diligence on other options.

Peter, and others after him, helped craft a sales process at Sonar6 that was just that, a process. As soon as a lead showed up in the CRM system, the sales team knew what to do. They knew the steps, right from first trying to make contact with a lead on the phone through to trying to close the deal before month's end. They knew what the different paths to purchase looked like and how to intervene at various points along the way. They also knew the math: the number of phone calls to get a lead to a first meeting; the percentage of leads that were genuine opportunities, not just tire-kickers; the likelihood of turning an opportunity into a customer. The team knew exactly how much activity was required to hit the sales target, and they could have a fair crack at forecasting new orders as well.

Realizing that sales is a process stripped back a lot of the sales swagger and bullshit, which was great. But here's the rub: Once sales was more transparent and accountable, marketing also had to step up. Salespeople are largely uninterested in marketers' talk of return on involvement, snackable content and immersive digital experiences. They just want leads.

If you work your way backward through the sales process, from the number of new customers a month to make target, to how many opportunities are therefore required, right back to how many leads are needed, then you're getting pretty close to a target for marketing.

Great sales and marketing organizations have sales and marketing departments that are responsible to each other. The marketing team commits to producing a number of qualified leads for the sales team. The sales team commits to turning a percentage of those leads into customers. Clear delineation of responsibilities works. Of course, marketing can have its fingers stretching deeper into sales, helping build content to progress leads and opportunities, but if marketing can't commit to a lead number it makes it hard to get sales to commit to a sales number.

We experimented with several variations of the division of responsibilities at Sonar6. In some territories we said sales reps could expect all of their sales to come from leads generated by marketing. In other territories we said that while marketing would provide some leads, salespeople were also expected to generate a percentage themselves from their networks, and from other ways of sourcing leads like LinkedIn or local business networks.

How marketing generates leads is part of your model. At Sonar6 we generated a lot of leads through outreach email and drip marketing, but it's all about what works for now, for you. One strategy isn't inherently better than any other; it's the results that matter — leads, and lots of them.

The biggest mistake is assuming that salespeople alone will solve the problem of lack of sales. Sales teams work best when they're drinking from a firehose of leads. I've already come clean that this advice is post-rationalized, but hell, I'll drag it out again: Adding salespeople to a broken marketing model is a bad plan.

Customers Are Your Business

"My CEO, he would stand up there like any other CEO and say that people were our most important asset. Imagine if, in one afternoon, people suddenly became your only asset."

From time to time at Sonar6 a customer would come and talk to the team. I remember this particular occasion so clearly. We spent the whole morning with all staff reviewing the strategy for the year, and we peppered the day with a handful of customer presentations. It was a great way to remind everyone of why, fundamentally, we existed: to help businesses better manage their staff.

Leeanne Carson-Hughes, general manager of HR for Christchurch International Airport, was speaking. We were scattered around the large wooden-floored foyer of the Sonar6 office, on beanbags, in armchairs and on Swiss exercise balls. Things had really started firing for Sonar6 by this point and we were already in our third office. What in previous iterations had been a typical startup's ragtag collection of furniture had now become more of an interior designer's idea of what a typical startup's ragtag collection of furniture should look like. In fact, the whole office had a funky skunkworks vibe to it. Furniture-wise, we could have been in any hot tech startup anywhere on the planet.

It was midafternoon, the graveyard slot for presenters. Everyone in the room had lost their morning enthusiasm, energy levels were dropping and the summer sun streaming through the wall of windows reminded us all that there was indeed more to life than HR software. Yet with that one sentence — "Imagine if, in one afternoon, people suddenly became your only asset" — everyone in the room was slapped out of their post-lunch slumber.

"After all of your buildings fall down, what else do you really have?"

Christchurch is a pleasant city of about 350,000 on the South Island of New Zealand. At 2:20 p.m. on June 13, 2011, Christchurch was struck by a catastrophic earthquake. Leeanne was doing her normal job, running HR for the airport.

Leeanne is one of those senior HR people who knows that businesses are built of people and who understands the inherent unpredictability of people. The sort of person who just doesn't buy your bullshit. She stood there in her smart suit, talking calmly, like she was narrating a documentary about something that happened to someone else, rather than a devastating event that she lived through. At times, though, her voice cracked just enough to show that, while she was a professional, and the earthquake was a true test of her vocation, her calm was still just a thin veneer over the raw emotion.

We were all captivated as she told the story. Of how, in a disaster, one of the first things that you need is to get the airport functional: Without it you can't fly in rescue teams. She told us about working with a team, many of whom didn't yet know whether loved ones were safe or whether they still had a home, and who were unable to get answers because the phone networks were down. And she talked of how those personal fears needed to be put aside as everyone focused on getting the runway open.

Leeanne's presentation utterly floored most of us. It was a stark reminder that our customers were real people. She went on to explain that over the next year they worked out of tents and with temporary infrastructure as they rebuilt. She even talked about how Christchurch International

Airport used our software during that phase. In that 20 minutes of speaking, Leeanne took us right inside her world and she became part of the family.

Customers really make your business.

Every customer you add should be celebrated in some way. I've seen businesses that sell enterprise software where deals are few and far between, and each one is celebrated with tequila. I've seen sales teams ring the sales bell to celebrate each new customer, and some days it rings every few minutes. I've seen consumer businesses with dashboards that show customer acquisition, and if the daily target is reached before 2 p.m. the whole team breaks into dance. I'm not kidding. Great companies are built around a culture of celebrating customers.

If Sales Is Shouting, Why Is No One Listening?

Jason Jones is a Northern California archetype. I don't know if he ever surfed, but you imagine that he used to, before college and kids and mortgages took over. He's laid back, with a gentle smile, but he also knows how to get business done. He knows perseverance counts.

I genuinely can't remember how we came to employ Jason, but I knew the instant I met him that I was pleased we had. He came on board to be our first U.S. sales rep when we were based in Santa Clara. Jason lived in Marin County, in the far north of the Bay Area. Because Santa Clara is at almost the opposite end of the region, he gradually encouraged us to move our U.S. headquarters north — first to San Francisco's Financial District, then eventually across the Golden Gate Bridge to Sausalito, just down the road from his house. That's good selling right there.

J.J., as he is obviously known, is a master of the *compelling event:* that moment in time when a customer has to make the choice of *"Am I buying something or am I not buying something?"* Sonar6 had a natural compelling event in that we were part of the annual performance-review cycle. J.J. was the expert at creating a compelling event out of thin air. Just like when you're at the car dealership and the sales guys goes and talks to his boss, then comes back and offers you a super special deal just for that weekend. A manufactured event to help close the deal.

I loved sitting in the office in Sausalito listening to Jason spin up stories to convince customers to buy sooner rather than later. He'd have a great anecdote for almost any objection. He had dozens of pithy reasons to get in early. He had contagious enthusiasm for the product.

All marketers should spend plenty of time observing the sales team, listening to sales calls. Salespeople spend so much time in front of potential customers trying to convince them to buy that they quickly explore every angle, and once they find the stories that work, they continually test and polish them.

At Sonar6 much of our most effective product marketing content was born out of observing J.J. and the other reps. It's arrogant to assume that as a marketer you'll understand selling better than a rep who does it all day. So go and watch. Learn.

On top of all the patter, Jason had a secret weapon. His goal was to "make HR famous," and it wasn't meant as a glib sales line. He genuinely wanted the customers who bought our software to be more successful as a result of that decision. He subtly helped potential customers realize that buying Sonar6 would be the best work decision they ever made.

And it worked. Maybe sales *is* a little bit of magic after all.

Startup Marketing Hacks #30-33

30. Sales isn't conjuring; it's a straightforward business process.
Demystify sales. Whenever anyone talks sales jiggery-pokery, call them out on it. Sales is largely an exercise in probability and perseverance.

31. Look for repeatability.
Understand the journey from identifying a lead right through to closing a new customer. Understand which parts of this journey are repeatable, and systematize those parts. Understand the math at each stage of the journey. Make sales predictable.

32. Make sales and marketing responsible to each other.
Marketing should be accountable to sales and sales should be accountable to marketing. Be clear that marketing is responsible for leads passed to sales and that sales is responsible for closing a percentage of those leads. Set a lead target.

Don't add salespeople to a broken model. If the business isn't hitting sales targets, be very cautious about adding more salespeople to try to fix this; you might just add more cost. Instead look at your marketing model and only add more salespeople when your team is drinking from a firehose of leads.

33. Learn from sales.
Salespeople are closer to your potential customers than anyone else in the business. Spend time with them. Listen to how they sell. Incorporate those messages in your marketing.

10.
Life's a Riot with Spy Vs. Spy[22]

The Money Booth

I once sat next to a pilot on a commercial flight. Not the pilot flying the plane — an off-duty pilot, flying back from somewhere as a passenger. We chatted. I wanted to know what it was like being a pilot and he wanted to know what it was like being an entrepreneur.

"Flying is 95 percent abject boredom and 5 percent abject fear."

---

[22] "Spy vs. Spy" is a wordless comic strip published in Mad magazine. It features two secret agents who are constantly using different booby-traps to inflict harm on each other. "Life's a Riot with Spy vs. Spy" is a 1983 album by UK artist Billy Bragg. It features the timeless lyric "I saw two shooting stars last night, I wished on them but they were only satellites, It's wrong to wish on space hardware, I wish, I wish , I wish you'd care."

"That's funny," I replied. "Being an entrepreneur is 95 percent abject fear and 5 percent abject boredom."

"Well, that's good, at least it's not boring."

There's one thing every entrepreneur I've ever met is a natural at: impression management. *Fake it till you make it.* Every founder of a business carefully curates the truth — they emphasize the joy of creation, of dreaming up a business and making it a reality. This is, of course, the most satisfying part of entrepreneurship. I distinctly remember looking around the office at Sonar6 a few years in and having this deeply satisfying feeling wash over me: This business that didn't exist now pays all these people; it's helping pay off mortgages, put kids through school, put the Sunday meal on the table.

But the flipside of that thought is pretty dark: What if it didn't work? If our projections were wrong or our investors lost faith, it would all crumble. This little flock of people would quickly be gone, trying to find other ways to pay their bills.

And it would be my fault.

I think fear of failure drives most entrepreneurs pretty hard. Couple that with an implied requirement to always appear fearless, and there you have it: the truly tiring nature of entrepreneurship. Elon Musk has said that "being an entrepreneur is like eating glass and staring into the abyss of death."

Funny enough, the thing that makes entrepreneurship so challenging is the same thing makes it so invigorating: competition. Building a business is a competitive endeavour. It's not about challenging yourself; it's about competing against others. All of the smart stuff you do to get customers is hard enough, but it's competition that makes it really challenging. It's easy to forget that any new customer you get is a new customer that a competitor didn't get. And vice versa.

Remember those game-show money booths, where the contestant has one minute in the booth with $10,000 flying around inside and they get to keep all the money they can grab? When there's no one inside and it's just the money blowing around, it looks so easy. But as soon as someone gets in there it's obvious that plucking the notes out of the air is, in fact, fiendishly difficult.

A competitive market is like being in a money booth trying to grab as many bank notes as possible, but instead of being in there alone, you're jammed in with half a dozen other people trying to do the same thing.

And then it turns out no one has trimmed their nails. *Everyone being successful is an economic impossibility.*

We Put Horses' Heads in People's Beds Because We Are the Mob[23]

The first hint I got that there was a problem was the text message on my phone: *London Sonar6.com, host failed to resolve.* It was autogenerated by the system that monitored whether our website was accessible from different points around the globe.

It was Saturday evening, the kids were in bed and I was waiting for the babysitter to ring the doorbell. Instead my phone dinged: another text. *Los Angeles Sonar6.com, host failed to resolve.* This was odd. There were now two places in the world where our system couldn't be accessed.

We were a software-as-a-service business. We held

---

[23] This is a paraphrase of the lyrics of "I Am the Mob" by the glorious Welsh band Catatonia. Yeah, I know it's an obscure song reference to an obscure movie reference used out of context, but it's my book, OK?

sensitive information about our clients' employees. A fundamental part of our product was that the data was secure and the service was always available. Our servers were in a bombproof facility in Texas with armed guards. We were built to resist any kind of cyberattack, and we had fended off several already without flinching. Security-wise, we had the whole shebang.

Yet here I was, on Saturday night, about to go out with friends, and the monitoring service was telling me that Sonar6.com was inaccessible from London and Los Angeles. The most logical explanation was that there was something wrong with the monitoring service. I got my computer out to log into the system to check, but before I could I got text messages telling me we were down everywhere.

I got hold of Mark. He was already investigating. Our servers were all still up, but our domain name was not resolving. It's hard to explain what this means in simple terms, but here goes: When you type the web address "Sonar6.com" into a browser, you're asking it to connect you to the Sonar6.com server. The browser figures out where the Sonar6 server is by going to a domain name server (DNS) — sort of like a phone book for the internet — to look up "Sonar6.com" and get its corresponding long string of numbers called an IP address. The IP address tells the browser where the Sonar6 server is, and off you go. Something in that chain was broken. Typing "Sonar6.com" no longer took you to our servers. It didn't seem to take you anywhere.

"I just don't get it," Mark said, sounding flummoxed. "It doesn't make sense."

I called around and got a handful of staff together to meet at the office. Saturday evening in New Zealand meant Friday night in the U.S., but even so I knew we'd need staff on to handle the calls and emails from weekend workers shut out of the system. No one really likes giving up their Saturday evening on short notice, but people did without complaint; it was that kind of business.

I'm going to cut a long story short here. It turned out that our domain registrar had blocked our domain name. Effectively it pulled our IP address off the DNS so that "Sonar6.com" just went … nowhere. In all of our security testing we had never even considered this scenario. The DNS service is such a basic element of being online that, once it was down, we couldn't do anything. We couldn't even receive email. Imagine this conundrum: Your service is unexpectedly down, but if you email customers to let them know about it you won't be able to read their replies.

Why had our domain been blocked? Right at the beginning we had registered our domain with a company that provided cheap domain registration services, and we never really thought about it again. That Saturday night we were cursing that decision. It turns out that when you're paying $10 a year it's hard to find someone to complain to. We did finally get ahold of the company; they lifted the block and we were back, although too late to rescue Saturday night. Our domain had been blocked because an unknown someone had informed the company that our site was involved in something illegal. In this scenario, their policy was to block the domain, *then* find out whether the accusations were true. We soon moved to a more expensive registrar.

So who had sent this nefarious complaint to the registrar? I'm certain it was a competitor. Remember, business is fundamentally a competition. Some competitors will do anything to win. It's an interesting question to ask yourself: Imagine you were down to the wire in a big deal and it was between to you and one other company. You discover an anonymous way to shut down your competitor's whole web presence for hours, possibly days. Would you do it?

Part of me got pretty shitty about this whole incident. A little because we hadn't covered this (now glaring) vulnerability, but mainly because someone did this, on purpose, to hurt us. That kind of asshole behavior was so foreign to our company culture that I struggled to realize a competitor could think this was OK. But part of me found the whole thing gratifying. We were winning deals against big competitors and they were hating on us. There's an energy there that we began to thrive on. Which was a good thing, because the more success we had, the more intense the competition became.

Winning Without Competitors Isn't Actually Winning

Competition is a sure sign you're in a real market. I often get young businesses showing me their business plans, and I always say "Tell me about your competition." Surprisingly often their answer is "We don't have any competitors!" Which means one of two things: Either they don't know enough about their market or they aren't in a real market. The world is pretty big. Almost every worthwhile opportunity has been sniffed out by someone. Sure, your competitors may look slightly different, they may be attacking the market from a different angle, but if you're competing for the same cash from the same customers, you're in a competition.

In the beginning at Sonar6 I think we were a little scared of competitors. We thought that being the only player "like us" was a strength, and that as soon as someone did something similar to us, some of our value eroded. But as we learned over time, this is the exact opposite of the truth. As usual we learned by looking at the data.

At Sonar6 we were religious about win-loss analysis. For every deal that a salesperson closed out, win or lose, we analyzed the sales process, including the competitors involved. Here's what we found: In about half our deals we were the only product under serious consideration. We called this choosing between doing something or doing nothing. These leads were considering either buying Sonar6 or continuing not to have performance-management software. For the other 50 percent of our deals, the leads were seriously considering several options for performance-management software. There were a bunch of competitors in the mix for them to think about, plus the option of sticking with the status quo.

We were surprised by what the win-loss analysis told us. The more competitors there were in the mix, the higher were our chances of winning the deal. The deals where we had no competitors were the deals we were least likely to close successfully.

Here's what we thought was happening. The customer had two decisions to make: First, to do something or to do nothing; second, if they picked "do something," to decide which product to buy. It seemed that more competitors working the deal meant more voices telling the customer they should buy some kind of HR software. In deals with lots of competitors, our competitors were doing some of the heavy lifting for us, getting our potential customers to believe in the product category. And then the Sonar6 product was so good that, once the initial "do something" hump had been overcome, it was relatively easy for us to win the deal. So it was actually better to have more competition.

Recently I bought a waterproof phone case. I had toyed

with the idea of a waterproof case for my phone ever since I got my first iPhone wet, and in the meantime I had damaged a few but had never bought a case. Why? Because it just wasn't a product category that ever managed to get into my "must-haves." When I went to the Apple Store I occasionally came across a tatty waterproof case in a forgotten corner of the iPhone cases display, but that was my only real experience of the category. Then one day I was at a large-format sports retailer and they had a whole wall of "adventure essentials" that included a wide rack of waterproof phone cases. Suddenly I was presented with several brands, in multiple categories: waterproof, shockproof, extended battery life and so on. Each brand had its well-crafted message for why it was the best, and the accumulation of those messages, as well as the sheer legitimacy that the whole "adventure essentials" display lent to the category, started a train of thought. I do lots of outdoor stuff. Maybe I did need a waterproof phone case.

Once I decided I wanted a waterproof case, once I was over that hump, deciding which brand I would choose was a much smaller decision. Some quick internet research and my mind was made up.

So there you have it — competition is good. Plenty of competition legitimizes a category for customers, and your competitors' marketing educates customers about the importance of buying a product in the category. In fact, I'd venture that the best markets in which to build a business are markets with several large competitors that are all a bit shit.

No, really.

Apart from benefiting from your competitors' marketing, there's a second reason competition is good: Competing makes you better. It's pretty obvious, right? Any runner knows that doing a training run and running a race are different things. The race will always stretch you more. We started Sonar6 in New Zealand — a pretty sleepy little market. But when we moved to the U.S. we made a conscious decision to locate in Santa Clara, because it meant we were right down the road from our biggest competitors, SuccessFactors and Taleo. This put us in more deals with more competitors — which we already knew gave us a higher chance of winning — and, more importantly, it forced us to raise our game. Continually coming up against well-drilled competitors makes you better, quickly. You refine your sales messages. Your marketing has to be more effective. And your general level of aggression, that desire to win? It goes through the roof.

The incident of the blocked domain name galvanized us at Sonar6. We started to hate our competitors just enough for it to be a good thing. But we also made a very conscious decision that we wouldn't compete by being assholes. We would compete by being better. We would win by having the best marketing, the best sales and the best product. Although it turns out that even that wasn't quite right.

Actually, You Don't Have to Be 'The Best'

I first spoke to Naomi Bloom from a tiny borrowed New York office. The speakerphone crackled and the air conditioner hummed loudly, making it hard to hang on her every word, which is what I wanted to do. Naomi is the doyenne of HR software. She has worked with multiple generations of HR software vendors, building a career based on both a firm grasp of how great software is built and an insistence that great business software must have a positive business impact.

On that phone call I imagined her as 6 feet tall and all

business. She quizzed me, quick-fire, on SaaS multi-tenancy, object models and other arcane areas of software architecture. Funnily enough, when I did finally meet her face-to-face she was quite different from my first impression: extremely bright, of course, but gentler, her intelligence equally engaged by talking about software architecture, old boats or whether middle-aged men should wear T-shirts. Also, she isn't 6 feet tall.

Anyway, the crystalline memory I have from that crackly phone call was a single comment. It may have been a throwaway line for her, but it had a lasting impact on our strategy at Sonar6: "The world is too big to be the best product," Naomi said. "The winners are the ones that know where they fit best."[24]

Let's think about this for a second. The idea that we needed "the best product" to win had been a fundamental assumption at Sonar6. But of course we didn't. You don't. There are plenty of examples of great businesses built on products that aren't best of breed. It's not about "the best product"; it's about your product fitting your part of the market best. So when I was ranting about competing by being better, having better marketing, better sales and the best product, I wasn't exactly right. Sonar6's success wasn't about being "the best." It was about finding our people and fitting *their* needs best.

I took this little gem from Naomi and we started to look at our market in a much more careful and granular way. We

---

[24] As an aside, the world is probably now too large for anyone to be the best at anything. While that statement breaks the logic of absolutes, it's still worth treating as true in case you ever get convinced that being the best is critical. As a grounding comparison, when Isaac Newton was the best mathematician of his age, his "known world" had about the same population as California has now.

asked ourselves questions like these: "What kinds of potential customers are out there? What do those different kinds of customers desire from their HR software? How well-placed are we to fulfill those different desires?" Basically we realized we would never be all things to all people.

When we thought hard enough about it, we found that, unsurprisingly, our product fit best for the sort of customers that we spent most of our time talking to. At that early stage this was New Zealand companies. New Zealand doesn't really do big companies, so by virtue of geographic location we were talking to smallish companies, fewer than 500 people. HR is important to most companies, but lots of them, especially smaller ones, don't value it as much as they should. Talent-intensive companies — business services, tech, creative agencies — tend to value HR more. So they were a receptive hunting ground. We built a product that worked really well for smallish, talent-intensive businesses.

Once we figured that out, we thought about what HR people in those types of businesses tend to look like. Those businesses would either have one overworked HR person, or, umm … a small team of overworked HR people.

We started to emphasize in our marketing and eventually in our product how we could help those specific overworked HR people. We showed them how easily Sonar6 could be implemented, how it would reduce their workload. And, of course, we characterized our competitors as likely to increase their workload.

This might sound a lot like target marketing but it's subtly different. It was about finding the places where we fit better than our competitors and then making our stronghold there. It became self-fulfilling. A client roster with lots of talent-intensive smaller businesses made it easier to attract more of the same.

This is the third great feature of competition. It diversifies and fragments the market, and, as this happens, the offerings from different competitors become more distinct. In this environment it becomes critical to understand where you fit, then to emphasize that fit over your competitors and to continually improve that fit, because as we know, having one group love you is far more important than having everyone feel a vaguely positive "meh."

Lead from the Front

Sonar6 was software, and software products really are something that you just think up. Software is made out of thin air. Across the whole cycle of founding a business through to being acquired, the time I'm most nostalgic about is the initial product creation.

Mark lived in a condo in a little cul-de-sac, and when we really needed to get through development work we'd abandon the beaten-up office on Nelson Street (with the leaks and the pizza boxes) and work in his living room. It was a bit quirky — there was, for example, a tiny climbing wall on one side — but it was warm, dry and quiet.

We started work every day at about 9, stopped at 2 for BBQ duck and noodles, then came back and worked into the night. It was a simple routine. We had a big list of programming tasks to get through and we just knocked them off, one by one, almost without conversation, except to either show off a new feature or work on a problem together. It was a hugely generative time.

I now realize the great luxury of that time was we had *no customers*. We were able to build a very pure product, unencumbered by pesky customers and their various desires. Our product went through three major revisions during the early years of Sonar6. Version 1, the version built beside the climbing wall, was a brilliant product. A simple idea, well-executed, with a clean purpose. Sure, we had done plenty of talking to potential customers right at the start, but after we distilled our ideas into a design we just went and built it.

By the time we built version 2 we had plenty of customers, and those customers were in the ear of the sales team, busily describing the features they wanted. The sales team, in turn, was passing all this along to our growing team of developers. Version 2 tried to meet all these "needs," no matter how poorly described, and the result was, candidly, a mess. Version 2 had more functionality than version 1, but it had become so hard to use that it lost its essence.

This was, however, a very valuable lesson. When we came to build version 3 we knew that we had to strike a balance between listening to customers and not listening to customers. At this point the customer roster was big enough that no single customer could dominate the discussion. Plus, we finally had enough market power and confidence to take customer feedback on board but use those requests to inspire and challenge us rather than to directly inform product development. Version 3 was a triumph. Customers loved it. In version 3 we didn't blindly follow what our customers said they wanted. We listened, we sifted and then we led from the front, presenting them with a product that fit the needs they expressed, even if it wasn't in quite the way they had expected.

For example, when we talked to HR people they often told us they wanted to be at the top table, to have more influence on the business. We took that insight and came up with a feature called Helicopter View. Employee performance reviews often were just a business process: Every employee completed their review with their manager, and that was the end of it. What we did was to take the ratings from individual reviews and create graphics that showed the performance of the whole business. At a glance managers could now see where the star performers in the business were and where underperformance might be hiding, and see the trajectory of individuals and teams. They could see that one business unit might be full of individuals where capability and output was improving year on year, whereas another unit might be stagnant. Businesses had managed performance for years, but they had never had access to this kind of information.

Helicopter View gave HR managers good talking points with their CEOs; we had made a feature that helped get them to the top table.

It's the Product, Stupid

Why am I talking nostalgically about product in a chapter about competition in a book about marketing? Because your product (or your service) is the essence of how you compete. The very first thing I remember learning about marketing at university was Jerome McCarthy's four P's. Apparently they still teach them: price, promotion, place and product. All startup marketers are product marketers at heart, and all marketers in startups need to tie themselves closely to the development of the product. As a marketer you ignore product development at your peril. Basically, if you're striving for the impossible dream of marketing — a product that sells itself — you need to be there right at the root.

Startup marketers need exceptional customer empathy. You should always be talking to customers and potential customers to understand what's desirable. What are the experiences customers value so much that they'll part with their money to get them? Then you need to get close enough to the people in the business who actually design and build your products to champion your customers' desires.

Remember, this isn't about asking customers what they want and then nagging the development team to build it, no matter how niche. (Generally that's a salesperson specialty!) This is about building customer insight, then using that insight to invent products or features that customers themselves would never have dreamed up but actually adore when they see them.

Nobody Expects the Naughty Hole

When my son Jack was 4 I showed him "Zoo Tycoon" on my PC. It's a game where the player runs a zoo. Gameplay includes terraforming the zoo grounds, building enclosures, filling them with animals and ultimately attracting paying customers to your zoo. Jack took to it quickly. He couldn't read much yet, but he could figure out the symbols and he knew his way around with a mouse. Before long he was building great big zoos on his own.

"What's that area over there, Jack?" I asked him, looking over his shoulder one day. He zoomed in on the map. The 3D landscape was thick with tropical vegetation. There were monkeys swinging from trees, colorful birds, lemurs. There was a waterfall and a cable car running through the enclosure, which was neatly fenced and ringed with landscaped pathways.

"It's the jungle," he said, beaming. "And over here is the snow." Jack zoomed out, panned across, then zoomed in on an equally impressive enclosure full of penguins, seals and polar bears, swimming in a vast lake or lounging on an ice shelf.

"Wow, Jack, that's awesome!" I was genuinely impressed. As Jack zoomed back out, I noticed an isolated area of intense activity in the top left of the map.

"What's happening up there, Jack?"

"That's the naughty hole."

"The what?"

"The naughty hole."

We zoomed in on that area of the map. Jack had used the terraforming tool to dig a very deep hole in one corner of the zoo. The very deep hole was full of grizzlies, lions, crocodiles, even a few sharks flipping around pitifully on the dry ground. And in among this throng of beasts was a handful of terrified-looking humans. These humans weren't enjoying the animals; instead they were being chased in tight circles, surrounded by the bloodied corpses of several apparently slower or less fortunate zoo-goers. It was gruesome.

I was bewildered. How had my darling son turned such a seemingly idyllic pastime as running a zoo into, well, the naughty hole?

"I don't understand Jack, what's the naughty hole for?"

"For naughty people."

"What makes them naughty?"

"Look, see." Jack panned back over to the jungle area. There were zoo customers milling around looking at the animals. They had different symbols above their heads that represented their mood. Happy faces, neutral faces, angry faces. The point of the game was to have a popular zoo, so the player aims to make customers happy by building exciting enclosures full of animals. But sometimes customers would get frustrated about a lack of bathrooms or about inadequate snack options. Then they would get the angry-face icon. Jack hovered the mouse over one of the angry people, who was probably unhappy about the lack of recycling bins. "Naughty," he said as he clicked on the person, picked him up, dragged him across the map and dropped him into the naughty hole.

I was flabbergasted. Jack had solved all the customer-satisfaction issues in his zoo by feeding unhappy customers to the animals![25] Apart from this being an interesting experiment in customer satisfaction, I was at a loss. I didn't know whether to applaud his creativity or scold his callousness. I was, however, sure that not a single one of the developers who designed and built "Zoo Tycoon" would have envisioned a player building the naughty hole.

One of great joys of building a product is releasing it into the wild and then watching what customers do with it. Once you release anything into the market, it's no longer entirely yours. This applies equally to your product and to your marketing. The market contributes to your business. You should not ignore that.

Another example: The Hong Kong Sevens is a seven-a-side rugby tournament. It's been running in Hong Kong since the 1970s. When it kicked off in 1976 there were 3,000 spectators; now there are 120,000, a stat that you might expect in a venture growing over 40 years. But it's the nature of just why the crowd is there that has changed most dramatically. In 1976 it was 3,000 hard-core rugby enthusiasts; today it's 120,000 people dressed in crazy costumes and out for a three-day party. How exactly this change came to be is hard to pinpoint. It was most certainly an evolution, but it's also most certainly a million miles

---

[25] And incidentally decreased his food bill as well, which is a significant expense for a zoo.

from what those initial tournament organizers in 1976 planned.

The customers have changed the product, and the marketers embraced that change. Much in the way that Wellington's Fashion in the Field is now part of horse racing, this colorful three-day party is now arguably the core part of the marketing for the Hong Kong Sevens tournament.

SMS, or text messaging, is yet another example. It grew far beyond what was ever envisioned for such a simple technology. Consumers grabbed it, made it their own and used it in all sorts of new ways, eventually spawning the messaging gold rush. Companies like WhatsApp and SnapChat were able to clutch onto the new behaviors that consumers attached to SMS, behaviors that had never been envisioned at the start of text messaging. Also, going back to gaming, young children use "Minecraft" to build huge imaginary worlds and share them with friends. This is now a core part of "Minecraft" 's marketing, but that surely wasn't part of the initial vision.

At Sonar6, part of our product let managers and employees set annual goals. This was standard annual-performance-review stuff — set a target for the year, then measure performance against that target. Because it was online it was easy to share these goals around the organization and to hold people accountable, which then spawned some of its own behaviors among customers: Rather than just setting big annual goals, customers used the system to set smaller, short-term goals. We hadn't really built the system for this, but the appeal of visibility and accountability of tasks outweighed the shortcomings of our design. Eventually this became a groundswell and we had to embrace it. We moved the product away from being an annual review tool and into being a tool that was used continuously to share objectives and show progress.

Nonintended product use is the sharp end of the wedge of market chaos. Let the market contribute to your innovation. Embrace your naughty hole.[26]

Startup Marketing Hacks #34-37

34. Competition makes things easier.

Rather than fearing strong competition, treat it as confirmation that you're playing in a worthwhile market. Embrace it.

35. Compete. For the win.

In most sales situations, having competition helps. Competitors share the burden of educating the market and of convincing customers they need to buy a product in your category.

Competing head-on will force you to up your game, and that is only ever a good thing. You always push yourself harder in a race than on a training run.

36. Listen to customers and don't listen to customers.

Winning isn't about having the best product or marketing; it's about matching up with your customers better than your competitors do. This usually means striking a balance between listening to customers and not listening to customers. Understand your customers' various needs and desires, then make a product that surprises and delights them with its elegance and usefulness. Don't get caught in the trap of adding one of everything anyone ever asked you for.

---

[26] Possibly the worst euphemism ever in a marketing text. I make no apologies; after all, it's better to be memorable than professional.

Yes, you're a marketer, but the product is the core of how you compete. Get close to the design and build teams and make sure the product development is driven by customer insight.

37. Embrace your naughty hole.
Once you have more than a handful of customers, you no longer own your product; you share ownership with the market. Look carefully at how the market uses your product and be on the lookout for any nonintended uses. They may well be the secret to future success.

11. Brushing Your Teeth While Eating Cake

Everyone Loves What We're Doing So This Will Be Huge

"You're from New Zealand? Do you know Anthony?" It's a feature of coming from a small country that people in other countries have this ridiculous notion that you'll know all of your compatriots.

"Anthony who?"

"Anthony Mitchell."

"Oh, yeah, I went to school with him."

Turns out that ridiculous notion is sometimes correct. Here I was, talking to a consultant in the lobby of a fancy London hotel and she knew my school buddy Anthony Mitchell — "Mitch" to his grammar-school friends. But Mitch is a lot more than just my school buddy. He's a strategist, a motivational speaker and one of the smartest guys I've ever met. He's also an optimist. I remember him describing a breakup with his university girlfriend with the phrase "the bed is half full." Clever, funny, optimistic.

That's my buddy.

Mitch was there when we dreamed up Sonar6. It's always good to get an optimist involved in your plans. Mitch generously shared his time and insight as Mark and I designed the first iteration of the product, and then helped Mark and me cook up the original Sonar6 go-to-market strategy: We would target law firms in Australia and the U.K. Why law firms in Australia and the U.K.? Well, Mitch's business, Bendelta, is a Sydney-based management consultancy, and it has many of Australia's top law firms on its roster. We talked to some of these friendly law firms and they told us they loved the product.

So our original strategy was this simple and this naïve: There were about 500 law firms in Australia big enough to use Sonar6, and the law firms we had talked to said they were willing to spend $30,000 a year on this kind of product. If we sold our product to 40 percent of them at $30,000 a year, that would be total revenue of $6 million a year in Australia alone. That would give us a great base to build the business from, but it wouldn't give us global reach, so we would quickly add the U.K. as well. On the surface the U.K. seemed to possess a similar law firm market as Australia, and there were plenty of them. Sounded pretty good. And it would have worked if it hadn't been for one thing: It turns out that a lawyer saying they love a product is a very different thing from a lawyer actually buying a product.

Mistaking expressions of enthusiasm about your product for potential sales is a rookie mistake. I'm guessing that being misled by expressions of enthusiasm is better than no one showing any enthusiasm for your product, but only just. Enthusiasm isn't cash. I love Ferraris, and can express fervent enthusiasm for them for quite a while. But I'm very unlikely to ever buy a Ferrari. There's the cost issue, and then there's how I would feel at the traffic lights. Despite my enthusiasm, a Ferrari isn't actually on the list of things I'm willing to pay money for. And someone paying you money is the only real sign of customer traction. Sure, there are consumer plays based on ad revenue and freemium B2B models where this rule doesn't apply, but they're exceptions. For the rest of us the proof of the pudding is in the paying.

In fact, even picking up a few customers doesn't really prove anything. A wise woman on Sand Hill Road once told me, as I spouted on about our handful of early customers, "Mike, there are 10 people in the world who will buy anything." She was, of course, completely correct. You only really know you have something viable when people other than the initial I'll-try-anything-once customers are buying your stuff. And you only really have a decent business, one that's going to seriously grow, once you start to successfully scale.

Size Matters

What is scaling? Clearly it isn't just adding more customers. In the early days of a startup you're adding more customers, but in a making-it-up-as-we-go-along and learning-how-to-do-it kind of way. Scaling successfully is when you add a lot of customers, fast, and relatively painlessly. To do that you obviously need to have a good product and a receptive market. We had a good product, I was sure of that. And here we were, Mark and I, in London with the management consultants who were going to connect us with our receptive market by taking us to meet some big law firms.

So, back to that fancy London hotel. Mark and I were staying there because the consultants were staying there, but the rates were more London-management-consultant than startup-from-New Zealand. I had called to make the booking and asked for their cheapest room with two beds. Unfortunately, the chap on the other end of the phone explained to me, there were only two rooms available for the dates I wanted, both with just one bed. Now, I would share a room with Mark, but sharing a bed was going too far, even for Sonar6. I muttered darkly down the line. In the end the chap took pity on me and offered a deal we could just about afford. He warned me that one of the rooms was very small, the other slightly larger, but said he'd give them to me at the same price. I vaguely relayed this conversation to Mark and he kind of agreed to take the smaller room.

Mark and I checked in and were shown to our rooms. My room was palatial. There's no other way to describe it. There was a hallway with a patio on one side and my own library with a fireplace on the other side. The hallway led to an enormous wood-paneled bedroom with a king-sized four-poster bed, and a spacious marble bathroom with what looked like a plunge pool. I'm not making this up.

"Slightly larger" may have been a case of English understatement. I was waiting for Mark in the lobby when I received this text: "OMG could you make a room any smaller?!" I went up to investigate. To start with it was quite hard to find his room. 236. That "2" meant second floor, right? Wrong. There was no 236 on the second floor. Nor was there a 236 on the first floor. Turned out that 236 was in-between, through a three-quarter-length door off the between-floors landing.

Mark let me in. He had a rough start. The room was indeed very small — so small that when he showered the bed was sprayed with water, as were the fresh clothes he'd laid out on it. To add insult to injury, as he stood there, naked and surveying his wet clothes, a double-decker bus pulled up. The people on the top deck got a perfect view through the window into his room.

"How small is your room?" Mark asked.

"Oh, it's pretty small," I said. I didn't really know what else to say.

For the next week, whenever Mark suggested we meet in my room I'd just reiterate that it was too small and that we should meet somewhere else. On the last day I think Mark got suspicious. There was a knock at my door and there he was, peering around me and down my hallway. Down my *hallway*! "Mike! What the fuuuuck?!"

As it turned out, London law firms were not a receptive market for our great product. Just like in Australia and New Zealand, everyone was very enthusiastic about the product, but getting people to buy it was hard to impossible. In Australia we usually found out in the first or second meeting if someone was never going to buy, because they told us. The U.K. was different. People were just too damn polite — instead of saying "no" they'd say "maybe" several times over until we finally got the hint. Eventually we did get some limited customer traction in the U.K., with a handful of clients on our roster (although none of them were lawyers). But scaling in the U.K. (and with lawyers) eluded us.

And actually, in hindsight, that was a good thing. When we went to London, Sonar6 did have a great product. But there was a whole lot of other stuff we had to do before we'd be ready to handle the pressure of adding a lot of customers quickly. That year shoveling shit for no result in London and Sydney kicked our collective ass, but the lack of new customers gave us time to put the business in order, so we were ready when we finally did find our market.

This book is, in large part, the story of our success

through optimism and muddling through. That approach gets you a long way, but it's not enough when it comes to scale. Scaling successfully requires more than a good product and a receptive market. You also need serious organization and quite a bit of math.

Think Smaller Before You Think Bigger

The act of learning while you grow in startups is so commonplace it has its own cliché: *Building the plane while you're flying it.* It's a nice phrase, but my absolute favorite way of describing the sheer joy of balancing discovery with growth is this one: *Brushing your teeth while eating cake.*

In the beginning there are so many things to be done immediately, and it often feels like everyone has to do a little bit of everything. That's totally normal. But it won't work when you come to scale. You need to think smaller before you can think bigger. By that I mean you need to break your business down into logical and manageable functions with clear roles and responsibilities. This sounds completely obvious, but it can be hard to do while also managing all the other must-do stuff.

Since Sonar6 was an internet-based software business, distribution and support for our product was relatively simple regardless of how many customers we added. The real challenge we faced was structuring a sales and marketing operation that could predictably generate, and then efficiently process, lots of customers. Of course, we also needed to ensure we could build a product in the first place. We needed to keep developing that product, and we needed to keep our subscribed customers coming back.

When Sonar6 was very new, my role involved product design, branding and demand generation. These were all marketing related, so they sat well within my skill set.

Product and marketing became my bailiwick; John took sales, implementing new customers as well as generally knocking on doors; Mark took on coding the product as well as supporting customers; and Pete, well, he took the rest.

This worked OK when we had our very first customers, but started to show problems when we could no longer count customers on two hands. The first problem was related to support and development. We had a very extensive product-development plan that Mark's team was responsible for, and that was heads-down intense stuff. Unfortunately, our growing group of customers using our first-generation product kept having support issues, and those issues were very reactive. If a customer forgot their password, they rang Mark (or someone on his team), and he stopped working on the important new product features to help them out. Proactive development work wasn't being done because customer support kept breaking the rhythm. The flipside was also a problem. If Mark's team didn't make a product-development milestone, they had the ready-made excuse of too much customer support.

So we moved customer support to my team. My portfolio expanded to demand gen, product design *and* customer support. Because this was the sort of role that was so confused that there was no standard off-the-shelf title (like sales manager or chief operations officer) we came up with the absolutely awful descriptor of "customer experience manager."

Even after this change there were still problems with who owned what. Mark owned building the product but not designing it, which was a rather unnatural break. John owned sales and most of our PR and community building, the latter mainly because I didn't have time for it because of customer support. Pete's team had started to be in charge of customer contracts, both renewing annual subs and moving our pilot customers into fully fledged ones. Customer satisfaction played a big role in his success, but I owned customer support. John had also started to hand over some of the implementation of new customers to a netherworld somewhere between Pete's team and mine, which created all sorts of bad first impressions.

It was dizzying.

I remember Sam Morgan, one of our board members who was not known for pulling punches, turning to the executive team one board meeting and saying "It's unclear who's responsible for what." Or words to that effect. Less polite ones.

Of course we all had our own responsibilities! Long lists of them, in fact. But when it came to those few key metrics that actually defined success or failure in the business, too many of them were shared. The business was simple. We needed to hit our sales target. To hit our sales target we needed to hit our leads target. To make money we needed customers to renew annually at our target renewal rate. Underpinning all of this, we needed the product to hit its development milestones or else we had nothing to sell.

Those four metrics became the solution to our problem. In the end it was surprisingly simple — each business function got responsibility for one metric. So there were four parts: R&D, marketing, sales and retention.

R&D was simple. It was a global function that designed and developed a product, deployed it and kept it running. Its metric was meeting the development road map. By putting all elements of product — from design to delivery — in the same place, then isolating that from the other distractions, it was easy to hold the R&D team accountable.

At a metrics level marketing was super simple. It was responsible for generating warm leads for sales, with a weekly leads target for each of the regions we played in. *How* we did that has been the subject of the past 10 chapters, but accountability to business was one thing: warm leads.

Sales turned warm leads into customers, also with a weekly target. Importantly, sales' role ended when the customer signed their contract. The sales team would have almost no contact with the customer again.

Retention looked after new customers. It made sure the Sonar6 software was implemented properly and that the customers were happy and would renew their contract each year. This included support, but that was a cost center. Retention was measured on recurring revenue — how much revenue we got each year from our existing customers.

From those early days of restructuring right up to when we were acquired, this separation of responsibilities was probably the single most important factor allowing us to scale. Teams got to focus on their part of the puzzle, everyone's work was measurable and we were all clearly accountable to each other.

This kind of structure we settled on is not uncommon in software-as-a-service businesses, but it's not applicable to all businesses. For instance, a professional services business would never separate the functions of sales from account management. An ad agency's business is built from relationships between account managers and customers that often start small and continue with varied offerings over years, so they can't separate that way.

Here are the key things to think about in structuring for scale:
- *Understand the base inputs of the business, the things you need to focus on to grow.* At Sonar6 the scalable inputs, the things that we could add to grow the business, were marketing

investment (more leads), salespeople (more deals) and engineers (build more features quicker). Retention was a little more opaque, but we knew retention rates were critical.

- *Make one team solely responsible for each key metric. One function, one metric.* If that's not possible, it's workable to have one function responsible for more than one metric, but vice versa is not cool. Never share responsibility for a key metric between functions.
- *Make functions accountable to each other, if possible.* Having marketing responsible to sales to produce the required leads felt great, and having sales responsible to marketing to close a percentage of those leads felt even better.
- *Split where the natural tension is and leave no room for excuses.* Giving Mark all of R&D worked because total ownership meant total responsibility. He couldn't blame lack of delivery on anything outside of his department. His team designed the product, committed to its own road map and then needed to deliver to that road map. Which is where natural tension comes in. If retention was expecting a feature that customers were demanding, or if sales were expecting a new product feature in order to hit targets, they'd bring pressure to bear on R&D.
- *Finally, don't be idiots.* All functions need to support each other. Sometimes things are harder in one department than in others. Be prepared to share resources.

How Many Suspects Does It Take to Make One Customer?

The fundamental equation of any successful business is this:

Lifetime Value of Customer > Customer-Acquisition Cost

The money you make from a customer must be more than the cost of getting that customer on board. Getting this right is absolutely the difference between a big business and no business. If you scale a business where the customer-acquisition cost is higher than the lifetime value of the customer (and if those costs don't change as you grow), you're just scaling up to a bigger and faster money-losing machine. Not ideal. Obviously then, before you start to scale you should have a reasonable idea about both sides of this equation.

Generally the lifetime value of a customer is calculated as the total profit from that customer over the length of time they keep buying from your business. In a subscription business like software-as-a-service or a magazine, the lifetime value of your customers is the profit you make from them each year times the number of years you expect they'll remain a customer. For example, people might subscribe to a particular magazine for an average of four years. If a yearly subscription costs $100 and the costs of producing and distributing the magazine are $85 per customer per year, the lifetime value of that customer will be 4 x ($100-$85) = $60. There are also lots of once-only businesses — tourism operators are an example. A business selling whitewater-rafting trips to tourists will expect no repeat business, so its lifetime value of a customer is the profit it makes out of a single rafting trip.

Now, as a startup, you haven't been in business long. So while you might know how much you hope to charge customers, understanding the length of time customers will stay with you is obviously problematic. At Sonar6 we knew our customers would pay us an average of $12,000 a year, but in the early days we really had no idea how long customers would stay. So we guessed: three years. That gave us an expectation of $36,000 of lifetime revenue for each customer. Once we accounted for our product costs (which were pretty low, being software), we estimated the lifetime value of our customers was $20,000. For our business to be able to scale, and eventually make money, we decided that we simply could not afford to spend more than $10,000 on acquiring a new customer.[27] Sales made $2,000 in commission, so we effectively had up to $8,000 for the marketing team to spend to secure each customer.

Let's look at a simple example: using Google AdWords to turn suspects into prospects (Chapter 6, if you need a refresher). Say we set up an ad that offers people who search for relevant keywords (suspects) some interesting content to download in exchange for their email address and permission to email them in the future. Once someone clicks on that ad and opts in to receive our content, they become a prospect. We send our prospects plenty of nurturing content and occasionally invite them to a webinar. Some of them attend a webinar and … bingo! We generate a lead. Great job, marketing! Hand the lead over to sales to close. Easy, huh? But before we celebrate I have a question: How much should we be willing to spend on each AdWords click?

We know we have $8,000 to spend on marketing to generate one customer. So what we need to know is how many suspects it takes to make one customer. Let's work backward, starting with turning leads into customers. Let's say our sales team wins 25 percent of the leads marketing passes along to them. That means we need four leads to get one customer. $8,000/4 = $2,000, so our budget is $2,000

---

[27] To learn more on setting acquisition-cost targets in subscription businesses, Google "LTV vs. CAC".

per lead.

Now, turning prospects into leads. Say one in 10 of the prospects we're busily nurturing with our awesome content actually attends a webinar, thus becoming a lead. That's not bad, but it means we need 10 prospects to generate one lead. $2,000/10 = $200. This kind of percentage is called a conversion rate.[28] So, at a 10 percent conversion rate we have $200 to spend to create each prospect. Remember, prospects are people who have given us their email addresses and agreed to receive content. That means they not only clicked on the Google ad but they filled in the form on our landing page and opted in to our database. That stuff has a notoriously low conversion rate. Let's say 5 percent. Twenty people need to click on our Google ad and come to our landing page before one of them will sign up. So, $200/20 = $10. Voila!

In this example, if you work the math backward you'll find it takes 800 suspects clicking on our Google ad to make one customer. We came to think of this as "funnel thinking." As in you need to pour a whole lot of suspects into the top of the funnel to get a few customers to drop out the bottom. Thinking like this, and doing the math, really tuned up the efficiency of our marketing machine.

Now here's the punchline: If the cost per click for our search terms on AdWords is less than $10, there you have it: profitability! If you want to grow the business, you just need to spend more money on AdWords, and you'll grow business value.

But if the cost per click is more than $10 you have a

---

[28] Collectively, these conversion rates and other calculations, like lifetime value, are called unit metrics.

problem. You'll either have to somehow revert to a different, less expensive marketing strategy or, if that isn't a choice, you'll need to cut costs elsewhere, with whatever pivoting that entails.

Oh, if life were that simple. There are, of course, complicating factors. So while it's immutable that great businesses have a lifetime value that significantly outweighs the cost of customer acquisition, there are several nuances that are important to consider when thinking about scaling.

Making an Ass

My first job out of school was working in a factory that made artificial plants. I'm not making this up. We would make these huge artificial ficuses and yuccas for office foyers using cut branches, fabric leaves and a hot glue gun. My boss was an old woman (or at least she seemed old to a 17-year-old version of me), and her favorite expression was "*Assume* makes an *ass* out of *u* and *me.*" I don't really know how it related to artificial trees, but it definitely relates to scaling a software business.

The first tricky element you should be looking out for is that even describing the math behind deciding how much money to spend on the cost per click was full of guesswork. We didn't know how long the lifetime of customers really was. Our conversion rates were based on the results we'd had so far, and because we were still new that meant small sample sizes. When you multiply lots of assumptions together, you risk making an exponentially large ass out of you and me.

It's actually even more complicated than that. We're dealing with probabilities. Conversion rates are just the probability that something will happen; they're not 100 percent predictive. In fact, we're dealing with probabilities multiplied by probabilities multiplied by probabilities — and some of those probabilities are just assumptions!

What does this mean? Well, it's a lot better than having no math involved, but you'll want a buffer. And you need to monitor and adjust all the time. Sound familiar? It should, because it's the same idea we used regarding being more scientific in Chapter 7.

The next trap is assuming the relationship between the amount you spend on marketing and the customers you garner is linear. The math we did above assumes the cost of acquisition stays the same regardless of how big you get, but this isn't always the case. One of the ways we grew prospects at Sonar6 was through list acquisition. We bought or rented lists of potential target customers and marketed to them. When we started these lists were cheap and performed well, but as we scaled we found the lists got more expensive and performed less well, so although our method was the same, the cost of acquisition increased. Sometimes the opposite happens. A lot of consumer businesses have to spend heavily on initial customers, but then word of mouth kicks in and acquisition costs start to fall. You get the picture.

A while ago I was working on the business plan for a nice business that does customer satisfaction surveys. The business was going well, and it had a great handle on its metrics. At the time the staff was in the middle of raising capital and one of the potential investors asked them to try an experiment: Double AdWords spend for a week and see what happens to the cost of acquisition. It was an astute question, because it turned out that doubling the AdWords spend didn't move the new-customer needle at all; all it did was double the acquisition cost per customer. Basically the more they were willing to spend, the more Google charged them per click. But interestingly, as time went on, without adjusting anything, the network effect of their surveys going out to hundreds of thousands of people took over and their cost of acquisition began to fall dramatically.

Caution: Most metrics in your business will not remain static as you scale. The cost of adding the first 1,000 customers might be quite different than the cost of adding the second 1,000. Just because you've got a formula that works today doesn't mean you've figured out how your business will be profitable forever — cost per click might go up or conversion rates might go down. Also, the opposite effect might be true: While you may not be profitable at first, you could see a way in which your increased scale or other changes would lead to profitability (or at least a lifetime value that's greater than your cost of acquisition). You need to monitor your actual cost of acquisition across your different channels, and you also need to be alert to, and ready for, how things will change.

The third and final nuance to all of this math and modeling is timing, otherwise known as *funding the sales cycle*. In our Sonar6 example we said that 10 percent of prospects turn into leads, which is very cool. However, we didn't say how long that took. Imagine, on average, that prospects have to be nurtured for 12 months before they become a lead. That number sounds high, but for Sonar6 it wasn't that far off. The implication of this, when you're trying to scale, is huge. In the example about the $10 AdWords spend above, we were spending all of our marketing dollars (apart from salesperson commission) on turning suspects into prospects, but those prospects might not become customers (give us money!) for a whole year. In the meantime the business had to find that cash somewhere. Marketing is an investment, but the return was a year away.

The upshot is this: As you scale you also need to keep a close eye on the sales cycle. Understand how long it is, monitor whether it changes and, most importantly, be aware that you may not see returns from your marketing investment for some time. This needs to be factored into how much cash you'll need.

Funnel Thinking

In real life you need to solve for a more complicated problem than just how much to spend on each Google AdWords click — you need to make trade-offs between all sorts of marketing options.

At Sonar6, knowing the conversion rates from our activities had a huge effect on our ability to make tradeoffs and invest our marketing funds wisely. As time went on we developed multiple ways of getting suspects into our customer funnel: AdWords, list rental, list purchase, sponsored webinars. We also realized that funnel thinking wasn't just for the internet, but could also be applied to our offline activities.

When we first started going to trade shows we'd justify the expense by having a target number of new customers out of the trade show. It might seem pretty dumb, but it's a surprisingly common practice. If it cost us $20,000 to attend, we aimed to attract two new customers, since our target cost of acquisition was $10,000. Which never happened (because, as the Active Path tells us, that's not how it works). But the beauty of funnel thinking is that it gives you a different way to look at the goal of any marketing activity, including trade shows. Now the goal wasn't to sign up two new customers; it was to generate 200 new prospects. Which was doable. A trade show is a pretty hard place to close deals, but it's a relatively easy place to get good opt-ins. Instead of designing a booth and organizing a show presence intended to close deals, we just wanted to get the attendees interested enough to give us their email address so we could send them, for example, an e-book on a hot topic (and, of course, further marketing content down the track).

If there were 1,000 attendees at the trade show, getting 200 prospects (a 20 percent conversion rate) seemed realistic. At a cost of $20,000 for attending the trade show, that's $100 per prospect. Which sounds like a lot as a bald number, but actually it's half the $200 we were prepared to spend to get prospects through AdWords. Funnel thinking tells you that the trade show makes sense. However, if we find that it's actually much harder to get opt-ins at the trade show than we expected and we only get 50, each prospect would then cost $400. Not good. Probably best to leave that trade show out of the mix in the future, unless you can make changes that you're pretty confident will lift the conversion rate from 5 percent to at least 10 percent.

At Sonar6 we were always in a state of brushing our teeth as we ate our cake. Over time our understanding of our funnel got more and more sophisticated. For example, we learned that prospects moved through faster or slower and converted at different rates depending on where they came from. As we figured out the details we adjusted what we spent on different types of suspect activity. We also added channel partners into the mix. The channel sales reps would identify leads out of their customer base and pass them through to our reps, and, since we knew what a lead was worth to us, we could easily tell if our spend in this area was good value compared with our own marketing efforts.

Don't Burn All Your Cake

Hopefully you get the drift. Scaling a business is inherently risky, so it needs to be done in a manageable fashion. You start by watching your conversion metrics, making some guesstimates, then refining as you go. You always need to keep refining. The more certainty you have on your metrics, the less risky it is to scale. You'll also need to put some buffer in the model, remembering that conversion rates are probabilities — they're predictive but prone to error.

As you start to grow you need to make sure your conversion metrics stay the same or improve. If you think they're not going to stay the same, you need to model that too. And remember that if you scale too quickly you might not have time to observe that getting your second 1,000 customers cost a lot more or a lot less than your first 1,000.

Time passes between when you spend marketing dollars and when that spending results in sales cash, so marketing is an investment. Part of your function as a marketer is to reduce the risk on that investment by, you guessed it, watching the metrics — in this case, the length of the sales cycle. And part of your function is to ensure that you invest in the right things. There are a multitude of ways to scale. You need good metrics so you can compare and apply your precious resources in the right areas.

What does this mean in real terms? It means you need to scale at a controlled speed — *at the same rate that you learn*. Every time you're able to refine a unit metric, you can accelerate, and every time you accelerate, you should be able to refine a metric. This doesn't mean that you can't scale fast; it just means that to scale fast you need to have a tight handle on the unit metrics.

Not to put too fine a point on it, but if you get this stuff wrong you not only don't scale, you actually risk losing everything. If you don't understand your unit metrics you can run out of cash and die — like of genuinely bad underlying problems such as your cost of acquisition being higher than your lifetime value, or through subtler problems you could have fixed, like discovering too late that the sales cycle was too long to sustain with your funding.

Metrics are hard and they're sometimes boring. But they're critically important to scaling.

There's a popular startup expression around scaling: *pouring gas on the fire*. I guess the metaphor is that your small business is a little flame, and to grow it you need to add fuel, but have you ever poured gas on a fire? Trust me — don't. It just involves everyone getting burned.

Instead scaling is about learning as you go. You're not pouring gas on fires. You're brushing your teeth while eating cake.

The Discipline of Distance

The main thing we learned from London was that it wasn't for us. The sales cycle was too slow, the U.K. took too long to recover from the global financial crisis and it was in a complete bitch of a time zone for a company based in New Zealand. For our team in the U.K. to communicate with our team in New Zealand in any kind of live fashion, someone would have to stay up all night. Somewhere in the world someone at Sonar6 would always be tired and grumpy.

We decided California was a better option for us, and a lot of what helped that decision was time zone. California and New Zealand are effectively only a few hours different, so there would always be overlap during working hours — five hours or so in the day when the Sausalito team and the Auckland team were in the office at the same time. The teams could communicate and learn together much faster.

I'm sure that all of the discussion about math and metrics makes it sound like this learning was all done as part of a rather clinical process, but it wasn't. In fact, a lot of what made us progress was very human! Frustrated phone calls between John and me in the middle of the night between the U.K. and New Zealand, trying to work out how to support a growing number of global customers without blowing out costs. The marketing team in New Zealand and the sales team in California working their collective asses off to crack the code of more sales, faster. The tireless Suzie and Elaine, who were responsible for client implementations, running through all of the iterations with the R&D team to make the product easier to set up. This is standard teamwork — working together, not letting people down — but it was the structure around it, the focus on metrics and repeatability, that meant we could scale.

Brian Sommer is a market commentator on enterprise software. He headed up Arthur Andersen's Software Intelligence unit way back before it became Accenture, he's done a startup and he's a contributor to ZDNet. He also has a haughty laugh, a Southwestern charm and a disarming way of distilling whole conversations into a handful of sentences.

"Do you know what your biggest strength is?" he asked me one frantic afternoon over a cup of awful coffee in a conference press room deep in the bowels of a gray convention center. I knew Brian enough to know that this was rhetoric: I didn't know the answer, and he did.

"You're 6,000 miles from your nearest customer. If something isn't right you can't just get in your car, drive over and fix it."

Brian was right. Scalable businesses depend on being built of systematized, repeatable activities. Being based in a country thousands of miles from most of our customers forced us to build the right kind of business. We didn't rely on bespoke responses to challenges, or throwing people at problems, because that wasn't an option. Instead we built something scalable.

Startup Marketing Hacks #38-41

38. Understand the metrics, then scale.

Growing a business is an exercise in balancing investment and risk. If you can't describe the math that ties marketing dollars to growth, there's too much risk.

39. Be organized: Think smaller before you think bigger.

Make the functions of the business discrete and accountable. Rather than throwing people at the challenges in your business, try to make everything you do repeatable and, therefore, scalable.

If you're building a global business, pay particular attention to how global communication will work, especially across time zones.

40. Funnel thinking.

A scalable business is one where the lifetime value of a customer is greater than the cost of acquisition of a customer. This is a fundamental business equation and, if you don't know how it pans out (or can't make a reasonably informed guess), it may be too early to scale.

Understand your funnel. How many suspects make one customer? How does this change across channels? How long does it take? Use the answers to these questions to set budgets and targets for your marketing team and to choose the most effective marketing approaches.

41. Over and over again.

Great businesses are always in a cycle of experiment, refine, repeat. You need to scale at the same rate that you learn. If you have enough understanding of how the unit metrics will likely change as you scale the business up a step then you can safely scale; and, implicitly, as you scale you should be able to better understand how those unit metrics will change when you scale up the next step. Like I said, it's a cycle.

This doesn't mean that you can't scale fast, but to scale fast you need to have a tight handle on your unit metrics.

12. Schmarketing

The Amplifier is Useless Without a Guitar
Right at the very start of Sonar6, Mark and I went on a business trip. We didn't taxi to and from the airport; that was too expensive. Instead we parked in long-term parking at the airport. When we got back we didn't go straight to the car. We loaded our bags onto a luggage trolley, then I climbed on the trolley with the luggage while Mark rolled it through the vehicle entrance back to the parking lot. The combination of the metal trolley and the extra weight was enough to fool the sensors into thinking we were a car. We grabbed the new entry ticket, raced to the car and were out within the five-minute grace period of the new ticket. Freeeeeeeeee parking!

Obviously that's dubious on a lot of levels, but that was the ethos at the start. Cash was precious, we answered to no one and speed was the most important thing. Oh, and Mark thought like an engineer. None of which is really about marketing.

Which brings us to the last hacks. I'm a marketer, and I know that so much of the success of a startup relies on marketing having its shit together. I've also talked about the importance of other parts of the business: sales, R&D, customer service. In the end, however, proficiency in these disciplines is necessary but not sufficient.

So here's the thing, marketers: Marketing isn't everything. It's an amplifier. It's the sizzle, not the sausage. If the underlying business is fundamentally good, good marketing can make it great; but marketing a business with poor fundamentals is tough or even impossible. No matter how much of a marketing demon you are, if the company is fundamentally flawed you stand zero chance of long-term success. This chapter is about some of the nonmarketing aspects a startup needs to succeed.

Don't Follow Your Passion. Follow the Cash.

"When did you decide to turn your passion for human resources into a business?"

"Errrrrgh, ummmmm. I didn't decide to turn my passion for human resources into a business."

It was an awkward interview. I was involved in a panel discussion at an HR conference, in a room full of HR people, and the host had decided to get the ball rolling by falling back on a common and dangerous myth — that passion leads to success.

In my first job out of university I got a corner office where no one could see my computer screen. So I played a lot of solitaire. The high point of my day was changing my computer's wallpaper, which I'd do every morning. And sometimes in the afternoon as well. I played in a band at night — *that* was my passion. My workday was pretty much just an exercise in wishing the time away while still getting paid.

The office paraphernalia I inherited included one of

those framed motivational posters. It's far too long ago for me to remember the picture (probably a grayish humpback surfacing in a faded sea), but I certainly remember the words: "Follow your passion, and success will follow you." A total crock, left as some kind of cruel joke. I quit my job to focus on playing guitar full time, because playing guitar was my passion. I had little to no success. Success did *not* follow me. Years later I started a company that targeted customers in human resources, something I had absolutely no passion for, and it worked. Clearly passion and success are intertwined, but not in quite the way that interviewer was implying.

Right at the beginning, before there was a Sonar6, Mark and I threw around a bunch of different ideas. We really, really wanted to build a successful software business, but we didn't pick the field we were going for by consulting our passions (racing bikes and playing guitar, respectively). Instead we thought about the passions — positive or negative — of potential customers. What was out there that people really hated that we could fix or really loved that we could make better? Eventually we came down to mobile phone gambling and HR software. People love gambling. They love gambling so much they get addicted to it. But at that time (2006) there weren't that many people using smartphones and it didn't seem a sure thing that within a few years there would be more smartphones than people on Earth. So we passed on gambling and moved on to our other idea: HR. People hate HR — specifically, performance reviews. Everyone you ever ask will complain about how horrible their company's performance reviews are. HR was a genuine pain point.

When I say "pain point" I mean an issue that's irritating enough that people would be willing to pay us money to get it fixed. There are lots of irritations in life that you kind of wish weren't there, but a pain point is different. It's so irritating that you actually pay to make it go away. Not all successful businesses are built on fixing pain points, but it's one way to engender customer desire, and customer desire is what all good businesses are built on.

Whether it's convenience (Uber), an irresistible afternoon treat (those cookies that keep showing up) or fixing customer pain (like Sonar6), your product needs to have an attribute that customers truly, deeply desire. This isn't rocket science. But it's surprising how many startup businesses fail this simple test. Sometimes it's because the business grew from some kind of really clever idea from a Ph.D. project, or something spun off from another venture. Sometimes it's just the misguided-passion error. The reasoning of the misguided startup founder goes something like this: "I love this. I mean, I really love this. Therefore, everyone else will too. Right guys? Right, guys?" Ummm, possibly. But unlikely. I've said it before: When it comes to business, customers' cash on the table is the only enthusiasm that really counts.

If you're going to put your life, your soul and your cash into something in the way that a startup demands, you're going to need passion to keep you at it. But having passion for a product that has no customer desire (like my guitar playing) is a "hiding to nothing," as the horse racing saying goes A passion for something that very few or no customers desire isn't the basis of a business, it's a hobby or an obsession or just a weird thing you do. Successful startups must include the element of passion *for being a successful startup*.

Actually, having a real need to succeed focuses the mind amazingly. When I left my corporate job to start Sonar6, I had a big mortgage and two kids under 3. The first members of the team at Sonar6 all had this sense of urgency that contributed to the success of the business more than all of our subsequent marketing smarts combined. We raised a limited amount of money and we needed to build a break-even business before it ran out, otherwise we were all screwed. It really was that simple.

The marketing team was the start of the funnel that ultimately resulted in sales. If we lost a day getting a promotion out late, that didn't just mean potential customers would flow in a day late, it meant they would flow out as a customer a day late as well. A day lost in marketing is a day lost in sales. Lose enough days in sales at this stage of the business and we'd lose the business. We got very fast, very fast.

When Mark and I started Sonar6, we had deep passion for building a business. For building software. For keeping our heads above water and not fucking up. People management was the field where we thought we could best express those passions. Along the way we realized what a great area HR is, and we did all become passionate about building software that made people's work life better. But we got into HR not because *we* cared about HR, but because other people — *lots* of other people — did.

Big Market, Big Chance

It's easier to be successful in a big market than in a small one. There's just more room. Of course, big markets are full of competitors, so it's hard for new companies to compete, and so on and so on, but there's just *so much more* room for success in big markets compared with small markets that all of those obstacles can be discounted.

When you think about your potential market, you should think about two things: how many people (or businesses) there are in that potential market, and how much each of them might be willing to pay you. That's the total available market: number of potential customers multiplied by the price they're willing to pay. In this equation the price people are willing to pay is really a measure of their desire. The worse the pain and the better your solution or the more incredibly lovable your product, the more it will be desired and the more people will pay for it.

When we were thinking about the HR option, we did some back-of-the-envelope math. We guessed there were at least a billion people who worked in jobs where they had some kind of employee performance review. All the people we talked to said their performance reviews were rubbish. We speculated that if we could fix performance reviews, businesses might be willing to spend $20 per person per year on our product. Times 1 billion people equals a $20 billion per year total available market. This assumption-laden equation was the basis of the launch of Sonar6. A big pain point multiplied by a massive market is an opportunity worth chasing.

If you have a big total available market, you only need a small bit of the market to be successful. In the Sonar6 example, if we were right-ish about the market size then securing 0.05 percent of the total available market would generate $10 million a year in revenue. That's a good place for a brand-new company to aim, and it seemed achievable. I sometimes see companies where their total available market is so small that to get to $10 million in revenue they'd have to get 50 percent of the market. That's just damn hard.

You can be successful even if there aren't a billion potential customers for your product, but you need to trade that reduced market size for more desire and more money per customer. For example, the number of people in the market for luxury cars might not be huge, but luxury-car brands succeed because of the high price they can put on customer desire. A startup stands a much, much better chance of success if it has a big total available market. Successful companies maximize the total available market equation: customer desire multiplied by the number of potential customers.

When Sonar6 was new we got some free advice from a management consultant who reviewed our business plan as part of a business competition. Under the section titled "Who is your target market?" we had written "Any business that employs people." We got roundly criticized. Apparently, as a startup, we should have been focused on a niche, but I like that original scattergun approach. Eventually we figured out that we had more success in small to midsize companies, and we were more loved by tech companies and professional services, but those were subtleties learned over time rather than distinct strategies. Sure, you might focus on a forgotten niche within a big market as a starting point, but bear in mind room to expand. Niche players can never be as big as broad market plays.

Animal Farm

All animals are created equal, it's just some animals are created more equal than others.

— George Orwell, "Animal Farm"

When I was a boy, my mother, in her charming motherly way, would use this Orwellian twist philosophy to justify any childhood inequality. When the adults got steaks and the kids got burgers, well, the adults were more equal than the kids.

It's a nice idea to think that all business success is simply a function of smarts, hard work and maybe a bit of luck.

That all businesses are created equal. However, it seems that some are created more equal than others. Aside from the dynamics of big markets and quality of competition, even aside from having a desirable product, some business types just have a fundamentally better business model than others, and a fundamentally higher chance of success.

Adam Miller is the CEO of Cornerstone OnDemand, which is the company that acquired Sonar6. By that stage my title was co-founder and CEO, and I had a wonderful group of people handling the different functions so I got to spend some of my time hanging out with the CEOs of other, often-much-larger software companies. What immediately struck me about Adam, in comparison with those other CEOs, was that he definitely wasn't a sociopath. Frankly, with many of the others it was hard to tell.

Adam started Cornerstone with a couple of other guys 13 years previous. They used to meet in a bowling alley in Santa Monica, and in looking at the early photos of the three of them there's a "Big Lebowski" vibe. What they did next is frankly astounding: building their way to a Nasdaq listing in about a decade, then becoming one of the 10 most valuable SaaS businesses in the world. Adam was always deeply involved in every part of the business, often down to the tiniest details, so a big part of that success must have been him.

Which meant that when I met him, I was expecting someone more hyperactive, or hyper-aggressive, or hyper-something, than the surprisingly unaffected and relaxed guy who met me at a borrowed San Francisco office to round out the deal.

We chatted about the business. I ran our well-rehearsed slideshow. He asked lots of great questions about the core team, about who did our creative work, and, in different words, about what we all wanted to do when we grew up. Eventually he started to get down to the things that really mattered to him: the business fundamentals.

He didn't want the hangers-on around, so we ditched his analyst and my business broker and we left the borrowed office and headed to an extremely noisy bar. This approach seemed nonstandard, but I lacked any comparators.

I realized later that Adam is a very human guy. (Can a human be nonhuman?) He likes to understand the people he's dealing with, to get to know them. I suspect he subscribes to the idea that *to recognize bullshit, nose is better than ear*[29], and when you're buying a business there's plenty of potential for bullshit.

Over beers, with questions half shouted and answers with no slides and no rehearsal, we had a wide-ranging conversation about Sonar6. Adam wanted to know lots of stuff. Cost of acquisition. Sales cycle. How cash flowed through the business.

And here's the thing: Some businesses *are* created more equal than others. For instance, some businesses just have a much lower cost of customer acquisition in comparison with lifetime value of customers. At Sonar6 we sold our product as an annual subscription. By the time we came to be acquired, we had an average customer lifetime of six years. Most customers kept renewing every year, paying us annually, almost without any intervention from us, for six years. Why? Once a business implements an HR performance product like Sonar6, it becomes a system of record. Customers just keep using it, and paying for it, without question. Getting new customers was hard and

---

[29] This quote is from the incomparable Toba Beta, the Indonesian economist and poet.

costly, but it's hard and costly for lots of businesses, including businesses where there's only ever a one-off sale, rather than a repeating revenue stream. Sonar6 was *more equal*.

Likewise, some businesses have a network effect that means once they get going, they don't have to spend much on marketing at all. Etsy, the peer-to-peer e-commerce website, focuses on handmade items. Basically if you buy or sell handicrafts, you know about Etsy. Etsy is *more equal*. Some businesses have negative working capital. When you get out of an Uber, your credit card is charged for the ride immediately, but the driver doesn't get paid for a few days. Uber is *more equal*. Also, unlike lots of businesses, Uber doesn't have any money tied up in carrying stock. Some businesses have very short sales cycles, so marketing investment gets an immediate return.

You get the point. The interesting thing is that you expect the economics of competition would balance these sorts of inequalities out eventually, so that no business would be just fundamentally better than others, and that does happen, *eventually*. It's just that eventually can be a long time.

So in that bar Adam, astutely, wanted to know what made Sonar6 better than other businesses, and most of the things that did were about our fundamental business model. Many of the elements that made Sonar6 appealing as a business to acquire were actually the fundamentals that fell into place when we first dreamed up the business. Some types of businesses just have a higher chance of success than others.

After a few beers though, Adam changed gears. He wanted to know everything about the people.

Food with a Story

It was the first Tuesday of the month, so that meant Food with a Story. The first staff member up on this day brought in two birthday cakes. He was telling the story of the cakes to the staff gathered around in the sunny foyer in Auckland and to the Sausalito team hooked up on the big screen.

"I'm adopted," he explained, "so every year I have two birthdays. When I was a kid, I had my actual birthday, the day I was born, and then we'd have my coming-home day, the anniversary of the day my adoptive parents first took me home." He started lighting the single candle on the top of each cake. "And it was a tradition that we'd have cake both days. Two birthday cakes a year. What more could a kid want?"

The Sonar6 people laughed and cheered, always appreciative of a personal story, a chance to learn more about someone, and of sharing food.

The next person up had cheese. "My father made cheese for one of the large dairy companies," he said, cutting the large chunks of cheese in front of him into smaller pieces as he spoke. "And he was always experimenting with how long you could age cheddar. When he passed away a few years back, the company kept his experimental cheeses aging, and have let the family go back from time to time to take some of the cheese." I think we all had goosebumps.

Sonar6 was an extraordinary place to work — a place where people shared their stories and laughed with each other, and supported each other when that was what was needed. Maybe I have rose-tinted glasses, but to me Sonar6 felt unique, fun, good. Extraordinary.

Food with a Story was part of a long tradition. When the team was still very small we had an all-staff meeting every two weeks where we'd talk about the overall progress of the business against our goals and celebrate new customers. A different staff member was responsible for making scones each week, usually with jam and cream. The meeting became officially known as Staff Meeting with Scones.[30] At some point as we got bigger and more diverse, someone pointed out that a lot of our staff members came from countries where there were no scones, so they were struggling to bake them when it was their turn! Staff Meeting with Ethnic Dishes was born. When it was your turn you brought food that represented your background. Russian, Slovenia, Indonesian, French, all parts of New Zealand and the U.S., Italian, Welsh, English, Malaysian, Filipino — we had so many different kinds of food, and, universally, people liked talking about the food they had brought. In fact, many of us looked forward to the stories more than the food, and eventually Food with a Story became part of the Sonar6 tradition.

Up third that Tuesday was Jackie. Jackie was a gifted and hard-working designer. I can't even remember exactly the food he brought, but I remember him explaining how, when he was a student, he had first come from China to New Zealand on an exchange program. For his final evening in New Zealand he had agreed to make some traditional Chinese food for his host family. But he had never cooked before, so it wasn't a success — in fact, it was a disaster. After returning to China and explaining the story to his horrified mother, it was decided that to prevent this shame from happening again, Jackie would complete basic chef training over his summer vacation. Jackie delivered the

---

[30] Scones are very English and normally are served at afternoon tea. They're similar to what Americans call biscuits. When Sonar6 still existed this scone information (and much more, including many recipes) could be found on the company wiki. We were quite scone-focused at the start.

whole story with such a deadpan charm that the whole office was nearly in tears.

I miss those days.

The final thing that separates great startups from the rest is the people: the capabilities they have and the culture they make. It's about having the team that can actually deliver on the strategy, and that's driven enough to do so, but that can also stop and appreciate each other along the way.

The first people we hired for the Sonar6 team set the standard. Urgent, of course. Generative. Smart. But also nice. People who you wanted to hang out with. Our culture was built up from that, and as each new member of staff was added we were very careful to find people who would enhance the culture.

The culture wasn't just about fun and support. People at Sonar6 got shit done. The right shit. This is the real requirement of a startup team. *There must be the capability to execute on the business plan. Relentlessly.* Startups require innovation, yes, but mostly they require execution. Day in and day out. At Sonar6 we needed a team that could build a kickass software product, market it, sell it and then service all of our customers. Anything anyone was working on had to pass a simple test: *If it's not going to help add customers or help keep customers, do something that does.* We actually had that written on a wall.

We were a technology company, so right at the heart of the company was a requirement for technical expertise. The founders all had a deep interest in how the product was put together. Mark and I built the prototype product ourselves. Later versions, however, were put together by proper programmers, much better programmers than either Mark or me. And that's another part of the puzzle that startups need to get right. The capability of the company needs to continually improve. The company needs to grow not just in numbers but in skills and competence.

Sonar6 did this in two ways. Firstly, we tried to always employ people smarter and more capable than us. Simple. That way the business would always get smarter. Secondly, we acted as if everyone at Sonar6 was there for work experience. By which I mean we all had so much to learn, and it was the company's responsibility not just to pay everyone, but to develop everyone. Partly to compensate for how damn hard we were working, but mostly because we had to. As we grew we ditched our old offices, going from a leaky hovel in an Auckland backstreet to quite nice, thank you very much, with an international presence. The team needed to keep up with the changes as well, but you don't break the lease on people and move on as your needs change; you bring them along and develop them. People management is hard, and I know we didn't always do this perfectly, but looking back at the Sonar6 marketing team, we all grew our skills, our confidence and our savvy as marketers.

Being at a startup is different. It's a group of people building something out of nothing. Startup people are poles apart from the normal corporate workaday stiff. They're not just the latest generation trying to keep a legacy alive; they're creating a legacy. And that legacy includes a culture that, like everything startup, is produced out of thin air. Voila! What fun! Food with a Story!

Keep Going

No one at dinner had been sleeping properly for weeks, and it wasn't just the impossible heat of an impossibly long Auckland summer. My phone was ringing on the table, face down, slowly vibrating its way toward my lap. As it breached the edge the lit screen suddenly caught my eye in the darkness of the bistro, breaking through my daze. I swung my free hand to grab it, throwing the red wine out of the glass in my other hand.

"Fuck, it's Dom. What does he want?"

I was with Pete, Mark and John, but I was talking to myself. I went outside to take the call. I wandered through the Thursday night throng outside the restaurants and bars, and dropped off the ridge down a quieter side street. It was so humid that the city lights appeared hazy in the near distance. My hair was damp with sweat, even though it was after 10. Dom was still at the office, and ringing me this late was not unusual — but what was odd was the endless small talk. He was nervous.

"Cut to the car chase, mate. How can I help?"

"I want to leave."

There was a long pause. No one had wanted to leave before.

"It's just getting to be too much."

I couldn't argue. The business was stretching everyone to the breaking point. But I did argue. That's what you do. You talk people off the edge.

After an hour on the phone my ear was hot. I went back into the restaurant. My food was cold. I explained to the others the conversation. Dom was head of support. We needed him. He would stay for another month, then reconsider, but he had had enough.

I actually felt like crying. I was already trying to keep so many balls in the air and I just didn't need to be searching for someone else to head up support. But being in a startup is like having a baby: No matter how relentless it gets, how hard, how repetitive, stopping is not an option. You can't storm off on your Segway.

Sonar6 was an idea dreamed up by a couple of guys who met cycling. When Mark and I started I had genuinely fuck-all idea about how to build a business. I had no idea how hard it would be. We worked day and night in a narrow, leaky office at the expense of everything else in our lives. When Sonar6 was acquired, we predictably had a huge party. We had champagne. Catered food. We even took the whole team sailing. It was an experience so far away from where we started that I never had dared dream it. In the middle of this celebration, a journalist rang me up. He asked me directly, "Now that you're a rich man what are you going to do with your life?"

"Well, I'm still working," I replied. I said that because I simply couldn't imagine anything else in my life. For all of the marketing smarts we learned and that I have shared in this book, Sonar6 was primarily about putting one foot in front of the other. It was about perseverance. I remember talking to my brother Philip the night Dom resigned, telling him how close I was to giving up. He summed it up: "Cry, laugh, do whatever you need to do, but just show up tomorrow."

We were a ragtag bunch. We made more mistakes than you could possibly imagine. But we kept showing up. And that right there is the final piece of the puzzle. You may not always know where you're heading, but keep heading.

Startup Marketing Hacks #42-45
42. Marketing is an amplifier.
If the underlying business is fundamentally good, good marketing can make it great. But marketing a business with poor fundamentals is tough or even impossible.

43. You need to have a passion for success.
Having a passion for being a successful startup is a critical part of being a successful startup.

44. Get the fundamentals right.

- *Big market, big chance.* Great businesses couple strong customer desire with big markets. They maximize customer desire times market size.
- *Find a business model that equals $$$.* Great businesses know their business model. They have a cost of customer acquisition that's a lot lower than the lifetime value of the customer.
- *Build a capable team.* Great businesses have a capable, generative team that's constantly improving.

45. Persevere.

Successful marketers stay the course. Regardless of setbacks, keep executing.

About the Author

Michael J. Carden trained in Artificial Intelligence but ended up spending his early career in marketing for global corporations. In 2006 he quit his cushy corporate marketing job to start Sonar6, a human resources software company with the sassy byline "At last, performance reviews that don't suck." When Sonar6 was acquired by one of its larger competitors six years later, it was the hottest company in its category. Sonar6 won numerous awards including PWC Hi Tech Emerging Company, Deloitte Fast 50, and Gartner Cool Vendor.

Now, Michael holds board and advisory board roles in various technology companies ranging from investor led early stage through to established public companies, as well as speaking and blogging on the ever-changing world of marketing. He is also a winner of the Writemark Plain English Award and the Bayer Innovators Award.

Michael currently splits his time between New Zealand and California. One day he'd like to be responsible enough to own a dog, but in the meantime he's helping raise two children.

www.ingramcontent.com/pod-product-compliance
Lightning Source LLC
Chambersburg PA
CBHW031622210526
45464CB00004B/1697